INCREDIBLE CHAMPIONS

INCREDIBLE CHAMPIONS

N. CHANDRASEKARAN

PARTRIDGE

A Penguin Random House Company

To order additional copies of this book, contact
Partridge India
000 800 10062 62
orders.india@partridgepublishing.com

www.partridgepublishing.com/india

CONTENTS

Dedicated to my daughter Sangeethaa

FOREWORD

Discussions on change at the grass roots and Corporate Social Responsibility or CSR as India Inc has come to call it, reflect a certain level of skepticism and at a few occasion even a sense of cynicism and despondency about the subject. Mainly because the belief is that the issues at hand are so large that it is not possible to make any noticeable impact on the ground. Bringing about social change requires champions many of them are not well known outside the realm of their small circle of engagement and more importantly there is very little written about the good work done.

Incredible Champions work is an interesting and well-thought effort by Dr. N. Chandrasekaran in bringing out various professionals who are contributing significantly to the society. He has been articulate enough to bring out the significant endeavors of these champions in different circumstances and been unique in their engagement.

This book will take readers through experiences and journey of the champions to illustrate and define the various issues of social sector in India. It explains how exemplary professionals see opportunity in challenging times and circumstances to serve a larger society. We may have heard individually about many of these champions. But a collection of chapters in this book serves well to inspire young minds as well as many others who are looking for opportunity to engage with a larger society.

Whether it is work of Narayanan Krishnan serving the destitute or that of Dr. Sai Lakshmi working for children from deprived economic community or that of Dr. Balasubramaniam serving the tribal for better health care and education, the objective remains the same—enabling the readers to relate to these examples and understand the concepts better while looking at development management professionals. Case studies are spread across age group, from professionals in early 20s to those who are in advanced stage in career. Similarly, number of years has not been used as criteria for choosing a professional to be profiled. But inspirational line of service and commitment has been highlighted.

The author has tried to cover all the important aspects of trigger to get involved in this sector, opportunities and challenges. There seems to be some common traits in spite of unique works. I am confident that readers would find it useful and will be excited to know how important it is to relate to the society. Moreover, as Indian companies focus on contributing to social capital for committing to "Corporate Social Responsibility of Business", I am sure this work could give enough pointers to look into.

I strongly recommend this book to practitioners of CSR at both individual and organizational levels and a great source of inspiration and affirmation to their own effort as well. My best wishes to the author and all those who worked together in bringing out this great book and I am personally looking forward to further editions that will cover a wider geography and more areas of work in the coming years.

Dilip Chenoy
MD & CEO
National Skill Development Corporation

PREFACE

My association with social sector goes back to times when I was a student at St.Joseph's college, Trichy. Trichy was the capital of Chola Kingdom for a substantial period of their rule. The place has an agrarian economy and depended upon river irrigation then. Thanks to the historical transpositions, town has excellent religious connections with different socioeconomic profiles. The town has been a centre of education then for a radius of 100 km where people would come-in to educate their wards especially for high school and college. The town has a cosmopolitan style, thanks to giant public sector that was started in the second five-year plan of India. As a student, my association in social sector started with relief activity on post flood management in the town as part of the college team. Those were the years when the river would flood certain low-lying areas around the town along with the banks. There have been a couple of years when we had heavy inundation damaging crops and life in the land of fertile delta region. I still relate a scar on my emotions when I lost my friend Manivannan due to flooding.

Since then, I wanted to relate my career to development management. I had my early days of research, scope to interact with renowned economists and researchers from the World Bank, Asian Development Bank and State and Central Government of India. I owe this to my association with the educational institutions and their focus. I had the fortune of working at National Dairy Development Board, Anand where I had exposure to length and breadth of India and interacted with many farmers and their family in downtrodden regions of the country. I used to engage my time with brilliant young mind on development issues.

It is here where I met great souls who are doing extraordinary professional service in social sector. There are generations of leaders created by this institution. Some of the professionals have moved places in the society including to work with business sector. I always had a carving to capture some of the good work done by my colleagues.

Recently, one of my friends who was associated with development sector died at a fairly young age. When I was pondering about him, I thought of writing a tribute which would inspire people. This must be a work on how professionals have looked at opportunities in social sector. Incredible Champions chose an area of work as they have a deep desire to touch others life with their vision and well-articulated plans of development work which is sustained over years. I am not trying to be prescriptive of "right" and "wrong" about people, organizations and system. The work focuses on the individual.

I have researched on every one of the champions discussed here. I have not tried to rank or relate in comparative terms. The choice of professionals is driven by areas of work I decided to focus on. Every one of them was approached based on the background of this work. They were listened to in person on what they have been doing and how they see it. All of them have contributed immensely to my knowledge and made me feel humble in life. I owe to them this book. If this book inspires and / or transforms the reader, the credit goes to the champions.

There was a structure put in place as I captured their discussion. Main ideas were to understand the trigger, opportunities, challenges and support they received in translating the vision into a programme or project. There has been a conscious effort to avoid credibility of investment and benefits. Though I feel social capital providers must engage professionals in developing and supporting with post investment management, this work is not focused on the same.

The work has tried to see commonality and uniqueness of each of the champions in their pursuit towards making life better for fellow humans. There could a number of sociocultural facets which are discussed but not intended to be prescriptive or evaluated for validation and adoption. The work is articulation of facts as represented and meant to be inspiration at best. This book can be enjoyed when the material facts are objectively viewed without any judgment on personal faiths and beliefs of people. The message is: Humbleness, Objectivity and Truthfulness in serving fellow citizens can make it meaningful. It is not awards and recognition but a sense of deep desire to make a difference is what drives Champions.

With this purpose, I welcome you to go through experience of these professionals.

N. Chandrasekaran

ACKNOWLEDGEMENT

I thank Mr. H. R. Srinivasan, Vice Chairman and Managing Director, Take Solutions Ltd for his continued support and encouragement on all my academic endeavors along with business requirement. Without his understanding and open-minded approach, this initiative could not have been accomplished. I thank Rev. Fr. Christie for his continued support in pursuing this work.

It would be appropriate to mention here the support I received form the champions and their office for this work. But for them, this would not have taken off. All of them are extremely kind and showered love, affection and a deep sense of cordiality. Thank You.

I would like put on record my sincere gratitude to Mr. S. Mohan, Dr. T.K. Nathan, Dr. R. Krishnan, Mr. D.V. Ravi, Ms. Madhu Vasanthy, Mr. S. Srinivasan, Mr. P.G. Subramaniam, Ms. Shobana and Mr. Ramesh G. for their guidance and comments on various issues connected with this work. I would like to thank Prof. G. Raghuram, Prof. P. Chandiran, Prof. M. Ramasubramaniam, Prof. Indira, Prof. Azaghu Perumal, Mr H. Sai Sridhar and Ms. M. Rammyaa, Research scholar from LIBA who have at different stages of this work been encouraging and supportive. I would like to thank Mr. Venkatesh and Ms. Protima Ghosh for their support in writing.

There a number of persons who helped me while I was researching on Champions and their work. Though I may fail to list all of them here, a few I would like to mention my gratitude to are Mr. Ashok K. Chordia, Mr. T.R. Nagarajan, Mr. Rajagopalan, Mr. T. Sreedhar, Mr. S. Sriraman, Mr. G. Muralidhar, Mr. Tamil Nambi, Mr. R. Ramachandran, Mr. Madhavan (Ekal), Mr. R. Srinivasan, Ms. Deepika (Student, IIM Ranchi),

Mr. N.Ganesan, Mrs. S.Srilakshmi, Mr. Badri Seshadri, Mr. Nandini Srinivasan, Mr. Albert and Mr. Ray Karan.

I am grateful to my mother Mrs. Annapoorani Nagarajan, my wife Prabha and daughter Sangeethaa for their continuous support and understanding.

N. Chandrasekaran

CHAPTER 1

Introduction

The "Incredible Champions" title is meant to focus on the contribution of a number of social activists in their chosen areas of work and location in which they operate. Over the decades, social work has been a proven area where a number of self-effacing individuals have made significant contributions to society. As a researcher, I always felt great curiosity to probe their triggers. I find that social activists are spontaneous: mostly, they did not choose to undertake social activity after receiving training in relevant areas of work. Furthermore, their ability to ignore personal monetary benefits makes the subject far more interesting to probe. There must be a strong innate drive, or things came about in the form of an outburst over an injustice, by sheer accident or through an unusual turn of events. Similarly, a number of other factors influence a person to focus on one or a selected few social issues and decide on a coverage area to deliver services.

As an analyst, I am interested in probing how such triggers get transformed into action plans. It is rather like building up a corporate or a for-profit company: social activists need to create a vision and build a strategy around that vision such that they can deliver action at the ground level. However, unlike corporate stakeholders, the stakeholders of a social entity (or even an activist) are heterogeneous, and could lack cohesiveness. Lack of cohesiveness usually arises because of mismatches between commercial and social costs and benefits. Often, social benefits could be appreciably high, but how does the social entrepreneur attract capital for such activities? Similarly, there could be conflicts between social capital provided for one time or for specific intervention and social capital provided as an investment meant to generate the kind of further capital required for a sustainable entity.

Leadership issues are also quite common in the social sector. An extraordinary individual reacts to a trigger and spends his or her life building an organization. How do such leaders develop the organization into a sustainable institution? This is probably the most challenging aspect of social ventures, as most of the times, the trigger and initial phase of development are more personal. As a more organized entity develops, the developing resources may not carry the same kind of intensely individual spirit. Though this book may not focus on this particular challenge, it certainly provides insights into the various challenges and opportunities that social activists and entrepreneurs face.

As we discuss leadership and succession, it may be important to understand the initial challenges for social activists, especially those who work on self-nurtured visions and are carving to impact their immediate societies. These challenges are some of the real issues a researcher would like to understand through conversations and other interaction. Many of us are moved by social issues, and want to associate ourselves with activities aimed at fulfilling the needs of the distressed, downtrodden or deprived sections of society. However, we would give importance to our personal priorities and shy away from working on social needs, which are less compelling. Given that natural tendency, it is to be wondered how these champions relate to social needs and are passionate about the same. There are different categories of such individuals who, as they turn into fulltime social activists, increasingly involve family and friends in their work.

Decisions for such dedicated persons are challenging, as they often have to sacrifice lucrative careers to pursue their dreams. This aspect is much more puzzling when the individuals become fulltime activists. Again, there are two categories of individuals here. The first category includes activists who chase their ideas and invest time, energy and whatever little money they have to create social capital. Using these assets, they build up an activity for a group of beneficiaries. The second category includes those few activists who join hands with other social organizations and extend significant support in building up current activities, adding new scope of work or adding new regions of operation. It may be important to note that both categories of activists give overriding importance to social activity rather than to creating personal wealth.

Some people do social work as a spare-time passion, along with their regular work. Social activity then becomes a secondary activity, but still, is just as significant. The rationale for such people to be socially active while working on personal income generating activities is their need to meet personal and family priorities. However, they also feel an urge to serve society. Here again, these are people for whom social activity is the major passion, while activities related to personal income are more a matter of subsistence and maintenance. These people also make for a supportive factor in terms of network building for social work. Some of them are well settled and have achieved a high level of contentment but want to be involved in social activities because it gives them the satisfaction of a comprehensive approach to living.

Of course, for such people there is a need to build and adhere to a scale of personal priorities in terms of pecuniary aspects and other non-materialistic activities, and relate them with their social activity interests. We are not just looking at private profit-making activities to give social gains but also at those people who have made conscious efforts to achieve social gains and have mapped their scale of personal profits/income on certain pre-defined requirements.

Here, we may note the importance of the value creation and value appropriation theories, which are widely discussed in social entrepreneurship research. Value creation is a primary condition for pursuing any economic activity. Value creation means resources deployed in an activity as input go through processes that add value to the output achieved. At times, value creation needs to consider both tangible and intangible costs, and benefits and surplus created must be greater than costs. Value appropriation is how resource agents share the benefits of value creation. The primary question is whether the value appropriation is fair and square considering the contributions of the resources. There is a tendency for some of the resource agents go beyond reasonable proportions given the size of their contributions. An unreasonable amount of income and wealth is commonly appropriated by project initiators.

Though value appropriation is important for the growth of societies and the economy, it has to be based on fair and reasonable means of sustainability in the economy. Furthermore, principles of justice and welfare must be established. Ideally, society would do well when the market economy achieves general equilibrium because resource allocation is efficient. This would be achieved when the aggregation of individual markets balances demand and supply of resource endowments. Value appropriation takes place based on resource allocation to value creation; there is scope for general equilibrium.

Though it may sound theoretical, social activists believe in enabling matching of value creation and value appropriation. When they start an initiative, there could be inequality in resource deployment or distribution of value created. This creates difficulties in attracting further resources. Furthermore, sustaining activities at current levels could be difficult. On the other hand, it may be a simple case of withdrawing resources from deprived humans, but not for reasons of misappropriation, theirs or anyone else's. Examples are those who fall terminally ill—the reasons are beyond their control. Social activists try to reverse the inequality of resource endowments and benefits by priming managerial effort and capital. A far more realistic way of understanding these issues is to see whether they achieve a balance or make an improvement over the current disproportionate distribution. If so, we will then have to see how we can encourage other social activists to pursue such noble goals.

The following points explain the private and social entrepreneurship options:

1. In principle, when there is scope for only low value creation and less scope for value appropriation by the promoters of the venture and its direct stakeholders, there is little scope for economic activity. If at all any activity occurs, it is more out of the desire to

hold on to a resource command. Over time, such resources can assume value. For example, a piece of real estate that a promoter and family were holding on to out of sentiment could have been giving poor returns. As urban agglomeration creeps into the locality, the resource would appreciate quickly and the promoters might appropriate the value, taking advantage of the changes in the economic environment. However, if one analyzes the fair return over the holding period, it could work out only to normal profits. In a similar situation, someone may have been involved in land speculation and made disproportionate wealth gains. This is in a different quadrant altogether.

2. This takes us to the next set of choices, namely, situations where there is low value creation but scope for disproportionate value appropriation by immediate stakeholders, mainly the promoters of the enterprise. This option is not welcome to social activists, as private entrepreneurs create unreasonable wealth because of their ability to manipulate the market due to better access to information, products and services. This is not a sustainable model as well. Once the deprived stakeholders become aggrieved, they revolt against the current working system or an entity. This leads to the next quadrant in the grid, namely, the thriving of commercial enterprises.

3. There are certain activities that ensure value creation for resource owners when deployed. They also set a suitable model for value appropriation that is closer to perfect market conditions, where resource owners are remunerated for their time and capital according to the proportion of value created. These are cases of sustainable and significant commercial entrepreneurship. This is where the project gains both economic benefits over costs and positive gains of social benefits over social costs. One can expect not-for-profit organizations and NGOs to be in this sector, provided they do not distribute profit among stakeholders but plough it back as social capital. Idealistically speaking, this is the quadrant and position social entrepreneurs should look for. However, some

benevolent funders and managers look closer at the quadrant where social gains are more than private gains or, to put it otherwise, the quadrant where social benefits exceed private benefits as intangibles and market distortions give better value for social gains.

4. In this quadrant, as mentioned earlier, social entrepreneurship gains importance over private benefits, as the latter are less attractive. For example, a benevolent person deploys prime property to generate funds for running a school under circumstances where operating costs are just covered because no market rent is charged. For this entrepreneur, the value of education to society is higher, and the forgone market rent is to be treated as intangible capital provided for running the school. Thus, social entrepreneurship arises more because of the need to address misdirected distributions of wealth or income as well as any other event that may lead to a distortion.

In this book, I have looked into social activists who are

1. individuals who are working on their own, while associating with other organizations as a volunteer or as an employee and
2. individuals who have started modestly but built up an organization of respectable size.

The domains they are working in include education—preschool, preliminary, secondary, higher secondary—vocational courses and selective higher learning; health care—medical, palliative care, hospice; environment—culture and activities aimed at the deprived, like differently abled people.

Generally, I cover the following in a chapter.

1. Early days—family, schooling and studies. Initial employment
2. Trigger: How did the person described get an idea? What were the moments that defined this happening?
3. What were the initial odds and how did the person feel about it? How did the person overcome these odds?

4. What is the role of family and friends in shaping up?

Typical target readers are

1. youth who would be motivated about the development sector;

2. management and engineering students who need to be indoctrinated on social leadership opportunities and challenges;

3. working professionals, who hit a plateau in their career growth and are looking at avenues for social work;

4. high school students who can go through the text for supplementary reading;

5. companies that will be into invest / spend on activities under "Corproate Social Responsibility" now after the new legislation. I hope they would like to have a framework on assessing individuals and projects. This gives data about individuals;

6. management students studying development management; and,

7. all those who are keen to understand social entrepreneurship and work.

The champions covered here are from Chennai, other parts of Tamil Nadu like Madurai, Tenkasi, Tiruppathur, Gudalur, Udhagamandalam, Coimbatore, Hyderabad, Ranchi and Thiruvanathapuram. I first decided upon the areas of coverage as the basic domains, as mentioned above. Then the first spell of research helped to generate a number of professionals whose work was validated by their networks of friends and professionals in the social sector. Though this is a judgmental sample, it covers a reasonable range of activities and beneficiary groups.

Since we are discussing triggers, opportunities and challenges, this sample set is likely to help readers arrive at a structured basis for such analysis. Furthermore, this would help the readers to understand how to provide for social capital providers.

There are certain possible commonalities while drawing inferences.

Trigger could be

1. an accident limiting a person and challenging his or her social engagement;

2. a genetic disorder that cripples a person;
3. an economic, social or cultural let down that forces a person to fight back;
4. a position of self-esteem and the desire to give back to society.

What is critical is the structure we arrive at after going through the chapters on all of these champions. Society needs more and more stimuli to be inspired to carry on such good work. The government's direction to plough back a small portion of the private profit of companies in CSR is proof of the need of the hour. Though this decision is right conceptually, it is important to do the appropriate monitoring and evaluation of people who can validate such social capital providers.

List of Incredible Champions

In this book, I have covered the following social activists, who most inspired me. I hope readers will find them interesting as well.

Champion 1:

Name: Arokia Anand
Broad Area: Social activist
Location: Chennai
Remarks: Born to a lower middle-class family and mentored by his grandfather to study, Arokia Anand could balance economic pressures and family values to ensure that he learnt the art of giving within his means. Arokia Anand fought a decisive battle to educate himself and now works in a large IT company in Chennai. His passion for social work was high from his early days, and he continues to associate himself with social work even today, along with his regular employment. Arokia Anand believes that the best way to serve would be to channel time and energy for the needy through a network of senior professionals in the domain and take their guidance in understanding and implementing meaningful interventions. If there is a contingency

by way of flood, fire or other calamity in any of the slums known to him, he is among the first few social entrepreneurs to engage with reconstruction of the lives there. He is the kind of inspiring youngster who wants to make a difference to beached starfish by picking them up and taking them back to water. It reminds me of a quote by Aesop: "No act of kindness, however small, is ever wasted".

Champion 2:

Name: Prabhakar J.
Broad Area: Social activist
Location: Tamil Nadu
Remarks: Prabhakar, who was born in Seetharamapetta, a village in Andhra Pradesh, showed great talent for line drawing, and all early signs were that he would become an artist. Even as a boy, his gifted pencil art won him accolades. He was very outgoing and service minded at school. He was disciplined and showed bravery in reaching out to social causes. He enrolled in the NCC and was an outstanding cadet. Through a sheer accident in life, he could not manage admission to an academic institution and further his ambitions of becoming an art teacher; he took a job in a factory at North Chennai. He resolved not to languish over spilt milk and to rekindle his interest in social service. There has been no stopping him since then. He proves that you do not need huge capital, but the willingness to work as part of a team and to network outside your own group to reach out to people. Sharing experiences and galvanizing interest groups have accelerator effects. That's Prabhakar, who inspires us. Prabhakar's work reminds me of Mike Dooley's quote: "At this very moment, there are people only you can reach . . . and differences only you can make". Developing a network and creating peer groups of social activists help accelerate good works.

Champion 3:

Name: S.S.Manoharan
Broad Area: Social activist
Location: Last served at Gudalur, Tamil Nadu, but has extensive experience across India.
Remarks: Manoharan was a very simple person. Even after spending time with him conversing on matters of common interest in social work, you would not have realized that he was a merit scholar as an engineer and a management graduate from a premier institute. He ensured that wherever it was not required, his education did not influence his natural personality. Very few people can sustain such simplicity. Here, I have focused on Manoharan as a social worker; I consider him a great champion. In my view, there could be any number of factors shaping his future and destiny. However, there are aspects of his personality I have observed and know well, which would make this humble person a champion in his own right. I would call him a "Leader in Own Terms and Style" (LOTS). He had different traits that are worth emulating by young professionals who seek to bring about happiness for themselves as also their immediate society in the ecosystem. I derived motivation to take up this work from him. Whenever I think of Manoharan, I am reminded of a quote, "There is no greater joy or greater reward than to make a fundamental difference in someone's life" (Mary Rose McGeady). He lived so!

Champion 4:

Name: S.Sreedhar
Broad Area: Social activist
Location: Chennai
Remarks: Often, a social service is rendered at an odd place, full of the downtrodden; the common man does not have the capability even to imagine such places or the plight. A powerful

trigger is needed to motivate one to render services to those who are otherwise uncared for and neglected. Some activists provide the service of giving final rites to those who die otherwise uncared for, whether by sheer accident, by coincidence of events in life or through deprivation. Some may die while they are under the protection of hospices. Sreedhar, influenced by the writing of Paramaachariya of Kanchi Mutt, decided to provide burial service for those uncared souls. He associated himself with old age homes and institutions serving destitutes. Later, he started a trust and pooled resources to extend this service to government hospitals as well. Even while holding a senior position in a private sector financial services company, he could comfortably manage doing this social work. To me, this makes him an Incredible Champion. I am reminded of the quote, "True peace is not merely the absence of tension. It is the presence of justice" (Martin Luther King). Sreedhar seeks justice for the destitutes' right to dignified final rites.

Champion 5:

Name: Jayanthi Ramesh
Broad Area: Education—Association with Anganwadi
Location: Chennai
Remarks: If you are well educated and fortunate enough to work in a well-established multinational company abroad in an attractive area of enterprise like information technology, the chances are you would pursue your career to reach greater heights. For a woman, the IT industry has proven to be a safe and secure environment that is more female-friendly in terms of leadership opportunities. Here, we have Jayanthi Ramesh, a person who could do all of this but decided on something else. If you consider the face value of the actions of this person, they may not be astounding. However, if you could realize the spirit behind those actions, you would be stunned. The path Jayanthi chose to follow was to impact children in her neighborhood. The little drops make an ocean. I am convinced

the world around us would be a better place to live in if only more professionals match what she has done. I relate her work to this quote by Benjamin Disraeli: "The greatest good you can do for another is not just share your riches, but reveal to them their own."

Champion 6:

Name: Padmini Gopalan
Broad Area: Education—Association with Balwadis
Location: Chennai
Remarks: What an amazing personality Padmini Gopalan is! While most of us start planning our retirement in our mid-forties in anticipation of our 60th year of age, here we come across a person who is in her eighties and had the passion to start social work at 72 years of age, when she decided to work for the good of poor children in her own way. She is an incredible champion who believes in meticulous work and follows simple logic when pursuing an activity, even as most of her known circle felt it to be impossible to make an impact in corporation (local administration) schools. She had such an impact that in due course, the local administration started training teachers adopting her experiment. It is no small achievement for a person of her background. Passion can help you make significant achievements if you are persistent. She reminds me of a quote by Martin Luther King, Jr.: "The time is always right to do what is right."

Champion 7:

Name: Shaikh Vazir E
Broad Area: Education
Location: Tiruppur
Remarks: Vazir, who had a humble if not deprived background, has fought impossible odds to establish himself economically by becoming an export-oriented entrepreneur in Tiruppur, a small

town in Tamil Nadu. He was a native of Udipi in Karnataka who moved to Mumbai, where he learned the garments export business. He now works with his partner to give back to society by supporting a kids' school and furthering the higher education of a selected few children. It may look trivial in terms of scope of social efforts. However, two aspects make it significant:

1. sensitizing his plight in a divergent society, by rising from a low-income group to establishing a value-based business, allied with the deep desire to engage with the ecosystem to help children from a similar background, and,
2. partnering with sourcing associates internationally and involving them in his social work by getting them to give positive contributions, especially when there were no economic or legal compulsions to do so.

Vazir is an incredible champion who has a deep-seated desire to make a significant impact over the years. I relate Vazir's work to a quote, "Diversity makes for a rich tapestry. We must understand that all the threads of the tapestry are equal in value, no matter their colour; equal in importance, no matter their texture" (Maya Angelou).

Champion 8:

Name: Satheesh Kumar
Broad Area: Education
Location: Tamil Nadu and All India
Remarks: Satheesh, who was born to a middle class, conservative family, went ahead to pursue his ambitions for serving society. He qualified to become a doctor in alternate medicine from Coimbatore. He went to practice in Arunachal Pradesh. After coming back to Udagamandalam, Tamil Nadu, as a college lecturer, Satheesh met his mentor and pursued his ambitions to educate

tribal children. His location in the Nilgiris District helped him to go ahead with this mission. Over the years, he has become a leader and mentor for many in the organization, and has been able to significantly impact tribal children's education, bring in more volunteers and work on the larger requirements of the organization. Satheesh is of the view that it is not necessary to think and plan on a big scale to carry out social sector projects. There is abundant scope to align with an existing movement in the specific geographical area in which one is comfortable. These great efforts from a person of humble beginning are worth emulating. To quote Oprah Winfrey, "I've come to believe that each of us has a personal calling that's as unique as a fingerprint—and that the best way to succeed is to discover what you love and then find a way to offer it to others in the form of service, working hard, and also allowing the energy of the universe to lead you."

Champion 9:

Name: G.V. Subramanian
Broad Area: Education
Location: Pondicherry
Remarks: India is a country with a lot of youth power; all demographic indexes support the concept of using this youth power for growth. However, the existing infrastructure and system are inadequate for effectively harnessing the potential of youth. G.V. Subramanian, born and brought up at Mumbai, was in a senior management position in the banking sector. He decided to work on developing a rural community college at Pondicherry where school dropouts could come and skill themselves. He helps to place all of them in the industry and service sectors. GVS's institution helps students who got stuck in their prime youth to rebuild their life. For a man to have sacrificed his comfort zone to pursue his dream is a phenomenal achievement. He is still humble; he is still crusading to expand his operations and

achieve a larger area of impact. Our society becomes a far better place because of the youth that champions like GVS harness, rejuvenate and inspire—both those who have dropped out of school and those who are pursuing high-end skills. I am again reminded of another quote, "Ignoring your passion is like dying a slow death . . . Passion whispers to you through your feelings, beckoning you toward your highest good. Pay attention to what makes you feel energized, connected, stimulated—what gives you your juice. Do what you love, give it back in the form of service, and you will do more than succeed. You will triumph" (Oprah Winfrey).

Champion 10:

Name: Shadab Hassan
Broad Area: Education
Location: Brambe, Near Ranchi, Jharkhand
Remarks: Shahid Shadab Hassan, who came from a humble background, climbed his way to a leading institute for his Master's in Business Administration and decided to dedicate his career to building up school education in his home village, 20 km away from Ranchi, the capital of Jharkhand. Shadab is convinced many of his friends lost opportunities to educate themselves and scale themselves up in life because of the fact that their access to schools was very restricted. He decided the best way to contribute is to make efforts to build a good school and encourage children in and around the village to study. In three years, he has created a large network, where even professionals from Google India, Bangalore, interacted with the students. Shadab is a remarkable youth worth emulating for his efforts to ensure education for the poor and for children of rural India. To relate Shadab's deed to a quote, "Life is either a daring adventure, or it is nothing" (Helen Keller).

Champion 11:

Name: C. Saravanan
Broad Area: Education
Location: Tiruppatur, near Jolarpet
Remarks: Saravanan was pained by the lack of opportunities faced by the poor in tribal areas and in remote rural villages. This affects society adversely, especially in terms of the local ecosystem, and the youth are caught in a vicious circle of poverty and low standards of living. A young Saravanan, in his early twenties, gathered the courage to work to give children impetus in their education through committed plans and efforts. One need not be educated and rich to conceive such social service. Mere deep thought, the corrosive absence of right mentoring and ability to receive supplementary efforts in studies can make someone act decisively. Saravanan, with a diploma in engineering, decided to give up his job to set up supplementary educational facilities in villages using local resources. He impacts tribal children and remote villages in this district. Saravanan is an incredible, self-effacing champion who makes a positive impact on his society. Saravanan probably believes in Robert F. Kennedy's quote: "Each time a man stands up for an ideal, or acts to improve the lot of others, or strikes out against injustice, he sends forth a tiny ripple of hope . . . and crossing each other from a million different centers of energy and daring those ripples build a current that can sweep down the mightiest walls of oppression and resistance."

Champion 12:

Name: V. murali
Broad Area: Education and Tradition
Location: Chennai and Tamil Nadu
Remarks: murali, a multi-faceted personality, has been balancing the requirements of a public sector job along with his interests

in the social sector. Over the last two decades, he has committed himself to helping children who are downtrodden and deprived in some form or other, mostly economic. Furthermore, he is interested in the preservation of 64 traditional arts of India, which are specifically located at selected areas as of now. murali, who again has a humble beginning, has been able to pool the support of colleagues and friends for a noble cause. murali's trigger to help the poor with education, Gow samrakshanam and preservation of Herbal Divine Star Trees came out of his struggles in his childhood. He swung into action on seeing deprived children, cows being sent to the slaughterhouse and rampant deforestation destroying trees. One can have a compelling reason to take up acts of social justice for which he needs to rope in friends and family; he must also have leadership capability and the ability to be secular and obtain support from multiple groups. It is an incredible effort for a man to balance the demands of family and work and yet act on his desire to be active in the social space! To relate a quote on what murali is doing, "Everyone has a purpose in life . . . a unique gift or special talent to give to others. And when we blend this unique talent with service to others, we experience the ecstasy and exultation of our own spirit, which is the ultimate goal of all goals" (Deepak Chopra).

Champion 13:

Name: Arun Krishnamurthy
Broad Area: Environment
Location: Chennai, Hyderabad and All India
Remarks: It is not easy to give up an opportunity to progress to a high-level management echelon in the corporate world, especially when the opportunity comes with the advantage of an early start to the career. Arun Krishnamurthy got an opportunity to work with Google India when he was younger than 20. However, a

strong desire to do something for the environment, about which he was passionate, made him quit his job. The willingness to forgo a potentially rewarding corporate career to follow one's passion and try to impact neighborhoods along with likeminded youth makes for rather brave and revolutionary thinking. The ordeal of convincing family and encouraging youth and children join him in his service was something he had to surmount. He did it by being a champion. Arun's work at a young age reminds me of a quote, "How wonderful it is that nobody need wait a single moment to improve the world" (Anne Frank).

Champion 14:

Name: R.Rajkumar
Broad Area: Health care—Blood bank
Location: Chennai and All India
Remarks: Voluntary blood donations and the role of organizations in mobilizing support are critical for the success of health care in an ecosystem. Rajkumar launched one such voluntary blood donations organization over three decades ago, and has since been managing it. The passion and commitment he demonstrates are phenomenal. He has done all this while working in a bank. His ability to connect people and institutions in pursuit of his mission is remarkable. It may be sheer dedication, commitment and charisma, along with the largesse of donors, which helped him achieve this. It is worth understanding how this incredible champion was fired up by a spark and has since been pursuing his social work, making it an institution. To quote, "Consciously or unconsciously, every one of us does render some service or another. If we cultivate the habit of doing this service deliberately, our desire for service will steadily grow stronger, and it will make not only for our own happiness, but that of the world at large" (Mahatma Gandhi).

Champion 15:

Name: Dr.B. Sailakshmi
Broad Area: Healthcare—Intensive care for pediatrics
Location: Chennai and All India
Remarks: When someone is born to a family of doctors, the probability is high that he or she would also be motivated to pursue a career as a medical practioner. If the person is materialistic, he or she person may focus on pursuing a medical practice of high-income value, apart from the professional satisfaction derived. On the other hand, if the person is altruistic, he or she may dedicate himself or herself to working in a community or public health system to serve the poor. Rarely does one come across a highly qualified doctor giving up her private medical practice to pursue her inner interest. In this case, the doctor concerned followed her heart to set up appropriate administrations and systems for providing health care to newborn children and babies whose parents could not afford intensive care to save their children from life-threatening conditions. This is about Dr. Sailakshmi Balijepalli (Sai) who, moved by her experiences with infants dying for want of medical care, decided to dedicate her life to eliminating this scourge. She reminds me of a Chinese proverb, "If you want happiness for a lifetime—help the next generation."

Champion 16:

Name: Khasim Shareef
Broad Area: Healthcare—Virtual network of donors of blood
Location: All India
Remarks: Khasim Shareef was born in a remote village of Andhra Pradesh. He had his primary and secondary education in the vicinity. Shareef commuted by bus over a long distance to attend school, and later, college. He walked miles to attend job interviews. He got a job in the IT industry and had an opportunity to work on

foreign soil for an attractive salary. He returned to India to balance the demands of his professional life with the demands imposed by the exemplary work he does in the social sector, work that touches millions of Indians. It is interesting to note how he nurtured his vision of serving the needy along with his technical capability and leveraged a network of friends to create a large pool of people who could donate blood on demand. Shareef's network for blood donation brings to mind the quote, "One person can make a difference, and everyone should try" (John Fitzgerald Kennedy).

Champion 17:

Name: Dr. R. Balasubramaniam
Broad Area: Health care, Education in tribal area and Development leadership
Location: Started at Western Ghats of Mysore, now in districts of Karnataka and All India
Remarks: Dr. Balasubramaniam (Balu) chose to commit himself to fulfilling the unfelt needs of tribal people right from day one of his qualification. Balu started Swami Vivekananda Youth Mission (SVYM) which has moved into a multiple activity. There is a 90-bed hospital at the original site and provides a number of extended services, including palliative care. There are more than 600 people now working for the movement. SVYM has moved into a number of activities such as education in tribal areas by running a school, academics in development education at Mysore, training and research, Indian studies, community development and so on. These efforts have received major recognition across the state and even in other states in India, and a number of policy and advocacy support measures are being provided. Balu travels across the globe talking on issues such as development leadership. He passionately talks about how failure to act on the elimination of poverty would be the most serious social crime. His conduct over the years has been phenomenal. He has managed an internal transformation that helps him look inward in solving social

issues and still be simple and avoid running after recognitions, rewards and the limelight. To relate a quote on what Dr. Balu is doing, "The great secret of true success, of true happiness, is this: the man or woman who asks for no return, the perfectly unselfish person, is the most successful"—Swami Vivekananda.

Champion 18:

Name: Fr. Thomas Rathappillil
Broad Area: Hospice
Location: Dindigal, Chennai and Chengalpattu
Remarks: When we look at death, life becomes meaningless. Fr. Thomas, who was born in a family of nine children, chose to serve as a priest and officiated in different parts of the world, such as France, Italy and Britain. After he had a cardiac intervention, he came back to serve in India. A turn of events made him start a hospice. He has subdued death by ensuring that destitutes who are kissing death are able to do so with peace and dignity. He is philosophical when he says that death equates all souls, whether rich or poor, men, women or child, healthy or diseased. It is important to facilitate people to take their final rest in peace. According to him, we cannot know the destiny of a soul after it departs. What we can do is ensure that it departs in peace. Noble is the thinking of Fr. Thomas, noble is the service rendered by him and his staff, and noble is his commitment and kindness towards neglected people. An incredible champion indeed! To relate a quote to what Fr. Thomas is doing, "The sole meaning of life is to serve humanity" (Leo Nikolayevich Tolstoy).

Champion 19:

Name: Narayanan Krishnan
Broad Area: Hospice
Location: Madurai, Tamil Nadu

Remarks: Naryanan Krishnan is a person who has received recognition as a real life hero by CNN. He has been featured on CNN Heroes—Everyday People Changing the World CNN IBN award. Born in a well-to-do family, he received a good education and started working in a five star hotel as a chef. He also got an opportunity to work in Switzerland, where an incident on the road with a destitute changed his life. He started pouring out his love and affection by serving food three times a day to destitutes on the streets of Madurai. Krishnan's deeds are heroic. He has charm, energy, leadership traits and the ability to fight against the isolation of people neglected by society in a small part of India. His mission is commendable, and is worthy of replication elsewhere. Additionally, Krishnan has the daunting challenge of sustaining his success in ensuring that there are no homeless people in Madurai district. An amazing personality! Probably one can relate to him the quote, "Never, never, be afraid to do what's right, especially if the well-being of a person or animal is at stake! Society's punishments are small compared to the wounds we inflict on our soul when we look the other way" (Martin Luther King, Jr).

Champion 20:

Name: Deepa Muthaiya
Broad Area: Hospice and Palliative Care
Location: Chennai, Tamil Nadu
Remarks: Deepa Muthaiya saw her grandmother, a doctor, serving poor patients with exemplary love and care. This became a characteristic of Deepa as well. But how she uses this trait in life to bring solace to people who are suffering is touching and commendable! It is not that she planned to do this from childhood. There have some triggers for her to consider hospice services and palliative care for those who are dying. This is a very niche service, as palliative care for terminally ill patients is challenging. Moreover, she is not a medical professional. She garners the support

of doctors and nurses day in and day out to offer this service. It is extraordinary effort to pool resources and extend this emotional and medical support, knowing that it is not going to be curative. For someone to switch from the corporate world to offering this social service is an incredible effort which is worthy of appreciation. I relate Deepa's zeal for social work with the quote, "Do not wait for leaders, do it alone, person to person" (Mother Teresa).

Champion 21:

Name: Bhageerathy Ramamoorthy
Broad Area: Home for destitutes
Location: Chennai, Tamil Nadu
Remarks: Imagine the plight of older people who are victims of changes in Indian culture and family systems. There are old age homes available to citizens who can afford them. However, not many people are that financially fortunate. Whatever the reasons, there are many single elders and even couples who have neither economic independence nor reliable support from their own progeny or siblings! Where do these people go to live out their remaining lives in comfort and with honor? It is common to see such people suffering without a proper home. Bhageerathy Ramamoorthy has long been motivated to do some exemplary work in addressing the issue of homeless elders, with the support of a few others. It is not that it happened overnight. She initiated work on this issue after getting married and being blessed with children. She started while she was working in a public sector bank. She is continuing to do it, with the support of family and friends, in an organized fashion today. She is a wonderful social worker trying to reach out to her immediate ecosystem in a sensible way and to be a champion for the homeless people in that system! To relate a quote to what she is doing, "As far as service goes, it can take the form of a million things. To do service, you don't have to be a doctor working in the slums for free, or become a social worker. Your position in

life and what you do doesn't matter as much as how you do what you do" (Elisabeth Kubler-Ross).

Champion 22:

Name: S. Ramakrishnan
Broad Area: Support for differently abled
Location: Ayikudy, Thenkasi, Tamil Nadu
Remarks: Ramakrishnan belongs to the category of unfortunate people who became physically challenged due to an accident in their prime. The level of impact and incidence vary from person to person. Though any crippling is a misfortune, there are cases where a person becomes confined to bed and a wheel chair because of spinal injury. There are some cases where victims are reduced to a vegetative state! "God forbid such cruelty" is a wish and a prayer. How does a family with a member who is so affected manage the misfortune? These victims must learn to refocus and rebuild their lives to achieve relative normalcy. We rarely come across a person from this category who not only restructures his life but also manages to set up an institution to serve other physically challenged people. S. Ramakrishnan, the founder of Amar Seva Sangam, who became a quadriplegic in 1975 at the age of 21, is an incredible champion and a great person worthy of adoration. I recall a quote, "Life is mostly froth and bubble, Two things stand like stone, Kindness in another's trouble, Courage in your own" (Adam Lindsay Gordon).

Champion 23:

Name: S. Sankara Raman
Broad Area: Support for differently abled
Location: Ayikudy, Thenkasi, Tamil Nadu
Remarks: Congenital muscular dystrophy often appears at birth with hypotonic and severe trunk and limb weaknesses. Obviously,

afflicted persons find it difficult to lead a normal life, as they are confined to wheel chairs. Like many other physically challenged people, they also tend to give up enthusiasm and the hope of being a normal human being due to the pains they undergo. This is an undesirable consequence, as they too have the right to lead a normal life. Here, we explore how Sankara Raman fought this kind of a physical challenge with courage, determination and intellect. He has teamed up with another champion whom we have discussed, namely, Ramakrishnan. The phenomenal character and spirit displayed by him, and his willingness to fight for ensuring dignity and restoring confidence in differently abled persons is worthy emulating. To relate a quote on Sankara Raman's efforts, "The price of inaction is far greater than the cost of making a mistake" (Meister Eckhart).

Champion 24:

Name: Raja Pannerselvam
Broad Area: Women and children
Location: Tiruppatur, Tamil Nadu
Remarks: There are people who encounter heavy odds in life at an early age for reasons such as accidents. When they survive such an accident, they find themselves at a crossroads on how they should handle their life going forward. Every now and then, we come across the rare person who fight great odds and dedicate himself or herself to meaningful social causes. Raja Pannerselvam was a school teacher who had an unfortunate accident that seriously impaired his normal functioning. However, his passion to serve society, especially women and children, made him start a home for them and gain recognition from the government. If you see him, you will understand the challenges he faces in running his home. He does it lovingly, with great spirit and dedication. He is an incredible champion for destitutes and women who have been affected by factors such as crime. I am reminded of a quote, "Do what you can, with what you have, where you are" (Theodore Roosevelt).

Champion 25:

Name: Jolly Johnson
Broad Area: Support to differently abled children and hospice
Location: Thiruvanthapuram, Kerala
Remarks: Jolly Johnson is one person who showed traits of becoming a social activist and started pursuing this line right from school, which was quite different from most of the students of her time. She showed an exemplary nature in donating a wheel chair to someone who needed it from her pocket money when she was at school. Now she runs a NGO named "Helping Hands Organisation" (H2O) with a vision to create a better world for the deprived and the needy; the special focus is on differently abled children. Jolly works on three distinct areas, namely, assistance for differently abled children, for destitute and for the ill, suffering in their dwellings. These services have come out of her conviction on the need to support people in distress. Jolly's deeds at an young age reminds of a quote, "Dare to be free, dare to go as far as your thought leads, and dare to carry that out in your life."—Swami Vivekananda.

CHAPTER 2

Saga of a salvation knight: Arokia Anand, Social Activist

Introduction: One may wonder how life unfolds for someone who is born to a poor family but is ambitious in wanting to make a difference. Occasionally, one hears a few success stories of slum dwellers taking up higher academics and demonstrating entrepreneurial talents and leadership skills. Similarly, there are success stories of how economically deprived people pursued their ambitions to land well-paying, responsible positions in different sectors like manufacturing and services. Some of these success stories help you to understand the kind of urge that makes a difference in spite of economic deprivation in achieving the twin motives of moving up the economic ladder and helping as many others as possible to do better.

Here is the interesting case of Arokia Anand, born to a poor family, who overcame all hardships to pursue higher education, and now works for an IT company. Over and above his personal achievements, the unique position he has adopted is to make a difference to the lives of others by extending whatever small support he can provide. He has taken this as his life's mission, and he believes that it would make him happier and more content. Incidentally, his economic well-being is linked to his work and his performance at his job. It is interesting to note how he blends the challenging demands posed by his involvement in both social service and professional work.

Early days of growth and role of mentor: Arokia Anand has an interesting family background that cemented his philosophies and his approach towards life. His parents were from two different religions, and encouraged their children to follow both. He belongs to a fishermen's community and lives in a housing board colony. His father hardly earned enough to afford a comfortable living for the family and education for the children. Though his father was respected in their community and he acted as the local head in resolving issues, due to economic conditions the family often could not afford two square meals a day.

Arokia Anand was educated by his maternal grandfather. Interestingly, his grandparents also were from two different religions and followed both. His grandfather used to take him along on visits to darghas, churches and temples, and talk to him about religious faiths and the need to be good to fellow humans, irrespective of religion. Arokia Anand noticed regularly that his grandfather was happy sharing his knowledge as well as his earnings for good causes. This observation had a deep impact on him. He learnt from his grandfather that giving is honorable and that when one gives whatever one can to a deserving person in need, it makes both giver and recipient happy. As a child and later an adolescent, this philosophy etched itself into his character.

Arokia Anand was educated by his grandfather, who put him in a school at Santhome in Chennai. His grandfather, who was alive until he passed the ninth grade, paid his fees all through those years. He was a tailor who stitched clothes for people living abroad. He used to get regular business from his customers. Arokia Anand felt the impact of his grandfather's commitment to work. At 70, his grandfather was hospitalized. His conditions required a private room, which was a luxury for the family. One afternoon, when Arokia Anand carried lunch, he found his grandfather cutting fabric in the hospital room so that he can start working after he gets discharged. This upset Arokia Anand and made him furious. However, he felt humble when his grandfather told him, "Life revolves around the belief that one will always return to normal from adverse circumstances and hence will have to fulfill all commitments to trusted customers. This is more important than pampering oneself!" His grandfather, his biggest mentor, did not live long after that. His final words made Arokia Anand realize that humility, selflessness and a sense of purpose—however small or big it may be—are important in life.

Holding on to purpose: Though Arokia Anand felt the impact of the loss of his grandfather, he pursued his studies with reasonable success. He was active as a scout; he was also in the NSS and was involved in many social activities. On completion of the 12th grade, he found new hope when he joined Patrician College of Arts and Science at Adyar, Chennai. This college was recently established: it was in its second year of operation when Arokia Anand enrolled for B.Com. there. On completion of his graduation, he sought admission for a post graduate course at Loyola College but was unsuccessful because of stiff competition. His morale sagged for a few days. However, he found new hope when he joined Madras Christian College.

Arokia Anand found motivation and worked hard at both academics and extracurricular activities. He was active in popularizing his college with the poor and middle classes as the college was fairly new and meant for the same target group. He took an active interest in blood donation camps and sports. He participated in athletics and won the 5,000 meters race. This period of three years taught him that one could make a difference to one's own place by bringing in positive energy, instead of lamenting on lost opportunities.

First engagement: After graduating, Arokia Anand wanted to pursue a Masters' degree in commerce. He opted to earn while he learnt by working with an NGO, the Centre for Child Rights and Development,

Chennai. Though the Chennai job market included a number of BPO job opportunities, he preferred to work with this NGO. He was doing social service by educating girls on adolescence and its impact on the grooming of their youth. This assignment required specific training in counseling. In two years, he completed his post-graduation and joined one of the top five IT companies. He worked in the night shift in the procurement department. Night shifts did not deter him from pursuing what he liked—to contribute to society.

Further involvement: In the IT company, he connected well with his colleagues by creating a fun team and involving himself in activities that gave him a sense of satisfaction. He established an identity for his team by naming it "Salvation Knights". This team helped needy people in small ways. It contributed money and purchased fruits and vegetables. Every Saturday, he took members of the team to spend time at one of the orphanages, where they made the children happy. He conducted shows, games and events; the happiness of the children elated him.

He spent a lot of time on demonstrating cleanliness and good practices to children, so that they could evolve and mature right. At times, he brought in guests (of some standing in society), and ensured that they celebrated at least one major festival with the children. These activities fulfilled his desire to bring about happiness in children.

He started working with Sreedhar (of Anatha Pretha Kainkarya Trust, a personality profiled in chapter 5 of this book) on arranging the last rites of people who died in homes for the destitute and of unidentified people who died in accidents and lay in the mortuaries of government hospitals. Arokia Anand explained that this experience was unique, as it taught him that life ultimately reduces to nothing. He remembers the words of his first mentor, his grandfather: "The best service to others is the offering you make without expecting anything in return. One day, life's journey terminates, and the soul must depart happy with having gone through the journey. While living, one may not experience this personally, but observing what happens around makes you realize the true sense of life". Arokia Anand sounded rather philosophical for a person of such a young age, but his commitment to making life purposeful for others rests heavily on his shoulders.

One of the strengths of Arokia Anand is his ability to connect with people and then stay tuned in. He is deeply involved in meeting professionals in the social work sector, and draws inspiration from them. When they give him an opportunity to serve, he joins them. Though this may seem to be an unfocused approach to others, he thinks that he is in the formative stage and needs to understand service without expectation of position, money and status. By involving himself with many others, he is able to see what path is right for him, where he could find the best experience of sharing his time and efforts.

He is also involved with Madurai Ilaya Pari, a social activist. He has approached Ilaya Pari as his mentor, as Ilaya Pari works on leveraging government hospital resources for poor diseased patients who often do not understand the benefits of approaching government hospitals, but instead allows themselves to languish. This may look like an odd activity, but it provides critical support for those who are seriously ill. This approach is of especial use for patients who are in the early stage of a disease. Arokia Anand supports Ilaya Pari in and around Chennai. Arokia Anand gets to go after more touch points for potential service. He has learnt to propagate optimal use of health care provided by government hospitals among the poor. This characteristic of Arokia Anand, of connecting with and attaching himself to resource persons so he can learn from them and then serve his immediate society is impressive, and needs emulation by others.

Arokia Anand also works with other social activists who provide care and support for AIDS-afflicted children. He finds this particular association special, because children get excited when he spends time with them. He works on this project during the weekends on a selective basis, as and when requests come from the two mentors, namely, Sreedhar and Ilaya Pari. Arokia Anand derives inspiration from working with these less fortunate kids.

Apart from these activities, he takes up some incident-based services. Sometimes, incidents those he has been familiar with occur, and he wants to make a difference in small ways. One such incident was when a fire broke in a house in North Chennai. Through his contacts at work and associations, for the affected children he arranged for notebooks, stationery and dresses so that the children could continue schooling without excessive worry. Though government and NGO support is available, he prefers to join in where he can add value. Simply engaging with the affected fellow humans and coordinating with them with all available resources is an invaluable morale booster for them.

Fundamental beliefs: Arokia Anand recalls the story of a person throwing starfish that had been swept ashore back into the sea while walking along the beach. Observing this, a friend comments that such an activity was a waste of time, because it could not solve the problem of large numbers of beached starfish dying. The benevolent friend picks up the next starfish and replies, "At least I can make a difference to this fish!"

Arokia Anand believes that whatever small difference he can make to someone that is worth the commitment is worth attempting. He is not worried about larger issues that are beyond his scope and capacity to address. It is a sensible approach, which most social activists pursue. Arokia Anand looks like a "rising star" because of his energy, commitment and willingness to fight, notwithstanding any adverse social and economic odds.

The other belief he has is that whatever one believes will happen, would materializes, whether it is good or bad. Arokia Anand wishes for and does meaningful acts in the social sense, and thus, benefits everyone associated with his acts.

He has a sibling who is doing a Masters in Social Work. His father encourages him a lot to be of value to his fellow humans. His mother gives him the freedom to choose his religious faiths and supports the concept of being agnostic about faiths or befriending all religions as a practice. Arokia Anand is married to his paternal cousin, who also encourages him to fulfill his commitments and in return, has the freedom to pursue activities of her choice. Thus, there is an understanding family encouraging him.

Conclusion: Arokia Anand is a young and energetic person with ambitions of moving up in the social strata. He would like to achieve a better standard of living. However, at the same time, he wants to devote his time and some part of his earnings to making a difference to persons who are deprived in some manner. His belief is that it is important for individuals and teams to gain satisfaction by doing social work in unison. Whether it is working for leprosy eradication, caring for AIDS patients and orphans or arranging funerals for unclaimed dead bodies, there are a number of formal organizations supporting these activities. Individuals involving themselves in these activities give some additional satisfaction to the needy and help make them comfortable. If more youths were to join with vigor in such activities, we would achieve a quantum leap in the average standards of living of the people of this world!

CHAPTER 3

Inspiring and connecting peers for a social cause: Prabhakar. J, Ennangalin Sangamam

Introduction: For the average man when he is young and energetic, social work as a way of life is the last choice. It is probably not on the list of choices at all. It is all the more difficult for a young man endowed with extraordinary talent. Normally, one would expect society to recognize such talent. It is natural to expect that opportunities would pour in for nurturing such talent and highlighting them to the world in ways that would make a material difference. However, there are instances we have come across of such gifted or endowed people staying unrecognized. This could arise because of many reasons, most commonly, it is for want of the right mentors. Some talented people may show the tenacity to fight it out and build on their talents. Others may divert their abilities to some other good cause and still prove themselves as being immensely valuable to society. In some rare instances, talented people have managed both to work for money and to get actively involved in social service.

When you get to know about the impact they have on society, you cannot but be amazed by their achievements. You would love to emulate them. One such person is Prabhakar, who has consistently raised the bar for humility while pursuing laudable work aimed at uplifting the deprived sections of society.

Early days: Prabhakar was born in Seetharamapetta, a village in Andhra Pradesh that is about 60 km from Chennai. From childhood, he showed great talent for line drawing, and all signs were that he would become an artist in that domain. Even as a boy, his gifted pencil art won him accolades.

Prabhakar was very outgoing and service minded at school. He was disciplined, and showed bravery in reaching out to social causes. He enrolled in the NCC and was an outstanding cadet.

These two facets of his young life, namely, his inborn talent for line drawing and his outstanding performance as a cadet in the NCC had him thinking of pursuing a life path aligned with either facet or possibly both. This author considers his life as a cadet outstanding, as he led his school in NCC activities and impacted his fellow cadets in all their exertions.

After passing his Secondary School Leaving Certificate exams in 1972, Prabhakar sought admission in colleges to specialize in fine arts and then take up a career in that field. You may call it destiny or bad luck, but Prabhakar was not admitted to any college, and his family circumstances compelled him to forgo his passion and pursue gainful employment to ease those circumstances.

In 1973, Prabhakar joined the Ashok Leyland Ltd (ALL) factory at Ennore as a fitter. He resolved not to languish over spilt milk; he would rekindle his interest in social service. He thought his excellent performance in the training as a NCC cadet at school would help him.

Here was an opportunity at hand at ALL factory, where there was a movement called *Nallor Vattam* (well-intended member circle). This movement was functioning under the guidance of Sivaram, its president.

Leveraging work environment: This forum leveraged the work environment and brought together a number of like-minded workers who could be associates in social work. Prabhakar used to take some socially relevant topics for discussion every week, and the group would arrive at plans for some action to initiate. These would be as simple as spreading awareness on issues like the ills of alcoholism, the benefits of a clean environment, safety, respect and established privileges and rights for women and the importance of maintaining good health.

Prabhakar asserts that

> The best way to engage with workers and their families is to go to their own dwellings and discuss the importance of leading a good and healthy life. This is quite basic in social work, something that I had to pursue meticulously. Initially, workers will not buy into such a movement, as they would be more preoccupied with day-to-day problems. Further, they lack the ability to visualize long-term needs. It is crucial to engage with them regularly and patiently on the virtues of uniting for a common purpose. One would face the challenges of abuse and resistance to such pep talks. But success comes in only when we increase manifold the group by voluntary associations.

The key lesson Prabhakar talk about here is the need to sustain interest in mobilizing all interested members with similar grit and enthusiasm for serving society.

Plans for a village: During this period of service, Prabhakar found a village that was about 5 km from Manali and not far from the ALL Ennore factory. This village required urgent attention. The village was afflicted with the severe problems of illicit liquor preparation and consumption. As we know, liquor consumption, especially by the poor, is not healthy, as it eats into their essentials budget and drains their energy. Hence, labourers who drink are not likely to be engaged gainfully or to earn a normal income. Their lack of income and indiscipline arising from addiction to liquor would have a downward spiralling effect affecting the well-being of their families, the education of the children and their social goodwill.

Prabhakar was deeply influenced by Mahatma Gandhi's philosophy regarding social service. He believed that the consumption of liquor was a serious impediment to a family's economic well-being. Hence, he continued to work to make his target audience give up liquor consumption. In the village Prabhakar found, the problem had more to do with illicit liquor. Alcohol is made in industrial units by the distillation process using molasses. Fermentation in breweries is an important process to make the alcohol potable. Industrial alcohol is sold as ethanol and methanol is mixed to make industrial methyl alcohol, used for making downstream products.

Poor people who cannot access branded potable alcohol for reasons such as lack of purchasing power resort to brewing illicit liquor. This was a rampant activity in the days of prohibition; unfortunately, illicit alcohol brewers have survived in many parts of India. They use low-cost chemicals of poor quality and undesirable methyl alcohol to lure consumers. Illicit alcohol can lead to blindness and death, as evidenced at many instances reported in the media.

Prabhakar and his team fought this trend as far back as the mid-1980s with *dharnas* and *sathyagraha*, forcing people to give up alcoholism. *Nallor Vattam* took the initiative by inviting Anna Hazare in 1989 to this village for an event spread over a day. This step impressed the villagers by introducing them to respected seniors who followed Gandhian thoughts. Anna Hazare duly emphasized the need to stay away from alcoholism.

In today's context, alcoholism is not considered that much of a taboo, since most Indian states have lifted prohibition. However, the ill effects of alcoholism are visibly prevalent, especially in communities of poor people. The problem is magnified when poor people consume illicit liquor to save on cost. When we consider this background, Prabhakar's effort is visionary. It was a Herculean task to start a drive against alcoholism in one small village and slowly spread it across many more villages through his network of social workers. He achieved a positive impact with exemplary courage, leadership and commitment, qualities that were later highly respected by the communities he served.

Serving through education: To get his intervention going in 1989, Prabhakar had to prepare well in advance by getting involved in a long association with the village community. He initiated his service by organizing a number of camps. These camps focused on issues such as health, eye donation and blood donation. Prabhakar's efforts started paying dividends when villagers started understanding wellness as a concept.

Village service became a routine activity for *Nallor Vattam* members. At this point, Prabhakar convinced forum members of the need to adopt the village for a major intervention. They started village visits and moved on to health care and education. In 1985, Prabhakar first organized educational support measures for students in the village. Ever since that first initiative, students have started to perform much better.

About 17 members of the forum under his leadership decided to contribute one per cent of their monthly salary to a corpus for setting up a school there. In three years, they saved Rs. 20,000 and launched a school at Manali. Now Prabhakar and his core team have set up about five schools across Chennai.

Prabhakar believed education is the key factor in the development of individuals and society as a whole. Hence, he and his forum members focused their networking activities on the provision and improvement of access to educational opportunities.

Changing orientation and moving along times: As the forum was sponsoring education, healthcare and environmental activities, Prabhakar wanted to participate in his own way in the celebrations of 50 years of Indian independence in 1997.

He used his natural skills to organize an exhibition of pictures drawn by him of 50 national leaders, to commemorate the occasion. The portraits were well received. Viewers included Dr. Abdul J Kalam, even before he became the President of India.

Prabhakar later arranged to hold exhibitions in different places. Encouraged by the response, he organized more concept-based exhibitions like "My Village" and "Clean Environment".

Looking at his artistic skills and his interest in socially relevant drawings, Ananda Vikadan, a leading publishing house in Chennai with several weekly magazines, offered to employ him full time. Prabhakar took up this offer, as it helped him travel to different parts of the country, mainly within South India. The publishing house wanted him to launch a new series based on the Purana Ashram series. This assignment took him to spots of interest such as the Bellurmath, Ramakrishna Pramahamsa's birthplace and Vivekanda's house.

This assignment proved again to be a turning point for Prabhakar, and spurred him to pursue something different. He remembers that he asked himself, "Instead of limiting my art to line drawings for social awareness, what else I can do based on the inspiration provided by traveling, visiting places of heritage and learning about the great Indian philosophers and social activists?"

Networking service organizations: In 2005, Prabhakar launched an organization called "Networking and Development Centre for Service Organisations" (NDSO). The objective of NDSO is to gather a number of individuals and small outfits that are doing great service to humanity through their dedication and commitment to social well-being. Most of these outfits are micro-focused in terms of geographical coverage. However, they carry exceptional learning potential, and demonstrate leadership that can be highly instructive for different types of outfits in the same region, in more diverse areas. Dr. Azhagar Ramanujam, a well-known social activist who belongs to the school of Vedathri Maharishi, is the President of NDSO.

Prabhakar has visited a number of villages and people who serve society. His vision was clear. He found it a challenge to unite these social entrepreneurs and bring them together in a forum where they could share their experiences. He started travelling to various project sites and visited the individuals who were the key providers of these services. This could be any individual engaged in constructive social work. Examples are individuals who go to village homes where someone has just died and convinces the relatives to donate the deceased's eyes. By 2013, he had arranged donation of 396 pairs of eyes. This was a great service to humanity, and other organizations engaged in social work can learn from him how to make such projects a reality.

This is the driving force behind Prabhakar's endeavour for *Ennangalin Sangamam* (Unification of Thoughts). This idea connects people in social work in such a way as to exponentially increase their collective strength and enable them to serve common causes better.

Recognizing youth on social work: Prabhakar deeply believed that youth who are pursuing social work must be inspired. He set up the Vivekananda Award in commemorate Vivekananda's 150th birth anniversary. He selected 120 people for the award. The criteria for awardee selection are that the candidate must be young, below 40 years of age, and must have achieved significant positive impact on society. The point was that Prabhakar felt the need to connect, recognize and inspire social workers and entrepreneurs. His efforts brought about a congregation of social workers who shared their experiences. He has also been conducting annual meets to which NDSO invites people for a day to share and celebrate their activities and success stories. This event has been held for the last eight years. The NDSO group has also started to clean up lakes in different places facing water problems. They cleaned up five lakes in Trichy, and have also done work at Dharmapuri and Chennai—areas where water problems were sometimes acute. These activities clearly show Prabhakar's carving to do something significant by mobilizing like-minded persons for a social cause.

In 2013, Prabhakar visited a village in Dharmapuri district, bordering Karnataka, as part of his idea for camps to identify and motivate 100 youths to revolutionize their villages. After hearing him speak, about 40 youths came forward and pledged that they would not drink liquor in future. As the matter got coverage in the media, the village elders also joined the youth and declared that the village would henceforth shun liquor consumption. Prabhakar and his wife Nirmala have resolved to celebrate Deepavali with the inhabitants of this village.

Ensuring family support: What is amazing about Prabhakar is his ability to win over people totally to any cause he is championing. This is a process that has to start at home. You may be curious to know how it went at Prabhakar's home when he took up a meagrely paid job at a factory and at the same time, started devoting his time to social work. After a while, he was married and later, blessed with two sons: Ravi Varma and Narendar. Interestingly, the names of his sons reflect his passion. This author was curious to know how he managed something that is not easy for the average man.

One can understand the drive that makes a worker take up unionism. Here in this case, however, Prabhakar had chosen a path of harmony in an aggressive labour-dominated industrial environment with tremendous success. The path he had taken was no flowerbed.

His wife, Nirmala, initially objected to what he was doing. However, he kept informing and involving her in all of his activities. Once a student from the village mentioned earlier, with the alcoholism and illicit liquor trade issues, came to his house to thank him profusely for enabling that student's success. This event moved his wife. She truly saw verifiable results of his hard work in transforming lives. She also became selfless and caring. Now, Prabhakar's wife is with him on all his social work and stands strongly behind his NDSO activities. Whenever she can, she travels with him to observe and understand the social work done by many others.

Conclusion: Here is a man who could not fuel his dreams and ambitions to exploit his innate skills for a gainful career but used the opportunity and environment for a larger purpose. Prabhakar uses his strength to network and his platform to convince people that the power of togetherness brings about exponential results in the social service sector if the objectives are meaningful and well intended. He uses his personality to augment resources and at the same time, is humble enough to stay firmly planted in the ground. In a world where workers may be hijacked by diversified ideological groups, Prabhakar sensed that harmony through concentrated group effort could bring peace and satisfaction to society. Prabhakar's story could make for a new model to handle industrial relations in factories, especially considering the necessity that today's organizations need to be "caring corporations" and to find harmony with their local environments. We could go a long way toward social-corporate unity if we had more Prabhakars!

CHAPTER 4

The unsung hero, simple, loving and resolute: S.S.Manoharan[1]

It was in May 1989 that my good friend Narender, who was my colleague as research staff at Indian Institute of Management, Ahmedabad, introduced me to Muralidhar and his friends. Murali and his friends lived at Anand, working for the National Dairy Development Board (NDDB). I often used to visit another friend of mine who was teaching at Institute of Rural Management, Anand between 1988 and 1989. That was when Narender insisted that I must visit Murali too.

I met Murali, Manoharan, Ramanathan, Tamil Nambi, Srini, Rajan and others, the list goes on. I saw some very common traits in all these guys—a high level of confidence, complete self-belief and extreme commitment to the cooperative structure (the Anand model). Each of them was raring to do something different that would enable him to impact society in his own way.

This chapter focuses on Manoharan, who I consider to be a great champion. In my view, there could be any number of factors shaping his future and destiny. However, there are aspects of his personality I have observed and known well, which would make this humble person a champion in his own right. I would call him a "Leader in Own Terms and Style" (LOTS)!

Manoharan was a very simple person. Just by looking at this man, you would not realize that he was a merit scholar as an engineer and a management graduate. He ensured that wherever it was not required, his education did not influence his natural personality. Very few people can sustain such simplicity. Whenever I met him, I noticed that his dress sense was always simple, reflecting his personality. His quality of not throwing the weight of his educational achievements and his intellect around was what made him different from others in the development sector.

The fact remains that simplicity helps not just to reach out to people but also to be available for them. Manoharan mastered the art of being approachable and making anyone comfortable when dealing with him. Simplicity is also an asset in problem identification. One can develop solutions to situations that arise as and when required, with whatever tools available. He had the unmatchable combination of problem identification instincts and ability to use his engineering and management learning to develop solutions.

There are other instances of his simplicity. His marriage to Durga was a simple ceremony. It was a very sensible act of avoiding excessive and vulgar spending on an event, which needs emulation by youngsters today! Manoharan was a person who believed that vulgar and unwarranted expression of wealth in situations in life is sinful. Though many development activists share this belief, there is often a large gap between thought and action. Obviously, practical demonstrations of inner principles in personal life situations are what can really be appreciated.

After I got married, my wife and I visited his home at Trichy to see his parents. I could relate Manoharan's life style to his parents' upbringing and the encouragement they gave him to exercise complete freedom in thinking issues out, rather than being emotional about them.

Manoharan had simple expectations in money matters. He had worked at the Market Intervention Operations scheme for edible oil in India when NDDB started it. I used to wonder about his masterly analytical skills and his ability to apply them to the cooperative sector. What was most interesting was his commitment to work for the co-operative sector. Had money lured him, he could have moved to the private sector in Mumbai, working for MNCs dealing in edible oil. In many discussions with me, he and his colleagues had profusely resisted even entertaining such a thought.

Some of us get attracted to the development sector when we look professionals working with institutions such as World Bank and ADB, which are big names in development sector funding. I could see in Manoharan a commitment to the development sector and a sense of pride in bringing about positive change through small and meaningful actions. To him, life was meaningful when you could make someone feel better. He did just that, and incidentally, he made a decent living out of it. If I do a valuation of his pecuniary opportunity losses, it would result in very high figures. What he really achieved, however, is hugely intangible. Hopefully, many more Manoharans will arise in the future. Sheer simplicity and commitment to purpose were the mantras behind his success in sustaining interest in developmental work.

After the tragic demise of a friend, Manoharan was deeply disturbed and wanted to work for tribal development. I was not sure why he was adamant, though he did give me the feeling that it was a call of conscience. Believe me, it was more than that! After a stint at Rashtriya Vriksha Mitra Sahyog of Anand, Manoharan joined Girijan Co-operative Corporation Ltd (GCC) at Andhra Pradesh. GCC was located in Bothili, Vizianagaram Tehsil at Vizianagaram district. He used to travel almost overnight from Vizag to this hilly place by bus. I understand it to be a scenic and beautiful place where he fell in love with the place and the people. For a person to move from Trichy to Anand and from there to a remote hilly small village was a big shift. I was wondering whether he would shift out of Bothili at some point in time. Such was his love and dedication for tribal development.

For most of us then, it felt like a weird decision, simply because we could not comprehend the way he looked at life. We think of life from a very materialistic viewpoint. Here was a man at the peak of his life, full of energy and dedication, who had decided to work in a serene and differently resourced location. In heart and mind, he was looking at facilitating the creation of economic value and peace for society. In the hierarchy of professional and monetary choices, education guides choices between long-term self-interest options. To emulate Manoharan, one needs a childlike heart and the ability to render truly unblemished service to the downtrodden. What one needs is a blend of simplicity, professional education, determination to create meaningful services that open the doors to decent living with pride, and peace within the self.

I regularly corresponded with Manoharan. I liked writing to him mainly to enjoy the pleasure of reading his replies. He had an amazing handwriting and excellent command over the English and Tamil languages. I loved his Tamil a great deal. I knew that he was in a place without adequate electricity. It was a hilly region that had no clean water source. I used to ask him why he wanted to live like this. He responded that people there loved him a lot, and it made him feel so good. In fact, he once went on a "sathyagraha" for four days to make men there more responsible towards their families and to get them to follow healthy habits like avoiding alcohol. I have seen such things on the silver screen and have read extensively about Gandhi. I am a great follower of Gandhian philosophy. I can relate proudly that Manoharan demonstrated the same Gandhian principles for the cause of the betterment of tribal humans. When I understood this, I thought God has been kind to someone doing some soul searching. However, my question to God now is: why were you so unkind to such a great soul?

After a few years of professional engagement with the Girijan Cooperatives at Bothili, Manoharan shifted to Gudalur to work for a NGO. Once again, he was leading a project for tribal area development. His wife was also working in the project. Their joint commitment was so high that their good work continued even after the arrival of his daughter, Vennila.

His team involvement and understanding was well depicted by one of his colleagues as follows: "He was our friend, mentor, guide and teacher. He held us all together for 16 years with his tireless commitment, and hard work". I used to be amazed by his unassuming ability to carry on with people for fulfilling tasks and willingness to reach out for any action at the ground. This would come only out of dedication to cause and not through education or training.

Manoharan loved music. He favoured light, soothing and meaningful songs with powerful lyrics. I remember him adoring songs sung by S.P. Balasubramaniam and composed by Illayaraja. Many of us are attracted to music. Manoharan, however, was one person who could lighten his mood and his soul with music, which enabled him to achieve peace in life. I had a few conversations with him when he indulgingly talked about songs and how he related to them. In his later years, he lamented the way the taste of youth had changed. He compared old songs with contemporary ones, pinpointing the changes that were at times not in good taste. These comparisons made me think of how much this person was sensitive to social factors, and how he related the influence of music to building character. I belong to his school of thought and sincerely feel that music can impact society both positively and adversely. It is the collective responsibility of society to keep the social fabric in the right condition. Good Samaritans like Manoharan may rest assured that their messages will be well received.

Manoharan was a person who always lent his support to a good cause. One of my friends wanted an Indian-born Australian girl to gain exposure to Indian culture and rural living, and to build character through a meaningful internship. Naturally, since her family was in Australia, they were seeking security, proper guidance and a liberal learning opportunity for her. This was a dichotomous situation where they wanted safety and protection as well as a liberal setting. I could only think of Manoharan and Durga, and wrote to them. I got a quick welcome note from Manoharan, in which he was nice enough to offer the girl internship at Gudalur. He then arranged for her stay along with his own family.

On their return, the girl and her mother were profuse in their thanks for the hospitality shown by Manoharan and his family. More important, the girl was taken aback by the kind of work they were doing, and she told me, "Money is a medium of exchange. The true treasure is devoting yourself for the well-being of the society around you". I do not know how much she was able to emulate Manoharan later in her life. I do think her voluntary internship became more meaningful because of her stint at Gudalur with Manoharan. Such was the impact of Manoharan's personality!

The other occasion when I observed his personality was at Gudalur in August 2007. I saw him after a gap of several years. Prabha (my wife) and I were on a holiday in Ooty. I called up Manoharan and told him we would like to spend the next day with him and his family. We were especially interested in meeting his little daughter Vennila. He welcomed me immediately, but advised me that we should join him for lunch and stay for some time thereafter, since Vennila returned from school at around 2 p.m.

We were there well ahead of time. He received us near his office at Gudalur and took us to his home. We had a great lunch and a fantastic time catching on with our Anand times and the days since then. Though Gudalur looked to me well developed compared to what I heard of Bothilli, his home was close to a grove of trees. He was pained to note my ignorance of nature and explained how reptiles and leeches are least harmful compared to human predators in the concrete jungles. Reptiles and leeches leave us alone if we leave them alone. I can understand someone born in a tribal area considering it normal to be around nature, but I was amused by the way my friend had adapted himself to nature!

During the short time I was with him, I observed his happiness at having built his own house in Gudalur. As I have noted previously, he was not into wealth creation. He believed money would be adequately available if one does good work. Wealth had never lured him. His view on building his own house was family oriented. Most of us in the development sector understand that family values are ingrained even when we work for a larger society. Only when the family's fair requirements are taken care of is such commitment to society possible. Here, I could see a perfect family man.

It showed in his love for his daughter Vennila! He was a proud father like so many of us. I could then see in Manoharan the traditional carving for and pleasure in sharing with the family. I could see that you can feel content in a life with meaning, without having to chase money and professional achievements. Manoharan and some other such souls have made me realize just how love one has for a daughter. That one day I spent with him has impacted me for the rest of my life. Manoharan is living in my heart and in my mind. It is like his own love for tribals, which needs to be experienced and cherished. Many cannot understand the sentiment and give it meaning without experiencing it! I do know that lots of downtrodden folk look up to Manoharan to give completeness to their lives.

I would love to write more about him, but I need to close this article, and I will do so quoting one mail communication I received from him after he fell sick. We had been discussing the hospital project that was on going in Gudalur. I had asked him to provide me with details like the project cost and gaps in funding gap. He wrote back to me saying that good souls must give by participating, rather than by fulfilling material requirements from a distance. A number of good-hearted souls were around to help materially, but the pleasure of participation was paramount. I had the pleasure of knowing Manoharan and cherishing his simplicity, commitment, intellect, humanity and love for self and everyone else. If God would create more such people, there would be no lack of humanity in this world!

Footnote: 1. Deceased in 2012.

CHAPTER 5

Respectful final rites for unknown:
S. Sreedhar, Managing Trustee, Anatha Pretha
Kainkarya Trust

I t is widely believed that a call to social service must have its trigger in deep observation, an odd experience or the influence of a mentor. Often, social service needs to be delivered at odd, out-of-the-way places most people never visit, to critically downtrodden people most people never think of, and under circumstances that may not usually be experienced by most people. Hence a powerful trigger is needed to motivate one to do unimaginable services to the uncared for. S. Sreedhar (58), a routine man of the world saw the trigger in an extraordinary book. The Senior Pontiff of the Kanchi Mutt—Shri Chandrasekara Saraswathy or Maha Periyava as he is revered by many, exhorting dharmic living, makes a passionate appeal in Vol. 3 of *Dheivathin Kural* to give a fitting funeral to the orphan who dies "unsung, unwept and unhonoured". When he read those lines of the Paramacharya something changed in Sreedhar permanently. As a result, many have benefitted from his extraordinary social service. Yes, Sreedhar benefits not the living, who may one day come to know of his help and probably record gratitude in return, but the dead who can never know who did what through the senses. And the theatre of action is the mortuary or the ghat.

One sometimes reads about unidentified bodies resulting from causes such as accidents or wanton efforts at self-destruction. And there are deaths occurring in destitute homes where it is not possible to trace any relatives of the dead to conduct the last rites. In the case of accidents, any dead bodies that remain unidentified after police investigation are preserved in mortuaries. Sometimes, bodies are brought to the morgue in highly decomposed state, sending stink to the high heavens. It is here that Sreedhar steps in, obeying the mandate of the Paramacharya. He takes all calls, from morgue assistants, police officials, railway authorities and from any passerby, at all hours. From here Sreedhar takes over and the dead, from now on, suffer no wrongs.

Early days at Chennai: Sreedhar was born and brought up in a village near Tindivanam, not far from Chennai. He came to Chennai for higher studies and to build a career. He and his cousin lived under the benign care of Kavi Yogi Maharishi Shudhananda Bharathi at Adyar. The urge to work for some good cause continued to burn in him. He read many religious works and the preaching of sages and scholars, which kindled his interest further. But *Dheivathin Kural* remained the most influential. Philosophically speaking, all humans are children of God, and no one brings along personal belongings at birth or takes them away at death. In a sense, all humans are orphans at all times, except for their transitory time on earth as humans. Sreedhar decided that he would work on arranging the burial of unclaimed bodies and the bodies of destitute, who breathed their last in homes run by NGOs. He first reached out to Vishranti, an organization for the elderly and the aged destitute, run by Smt. Savitri Vaithi. According to Sreedhar "the idea is to arrange funerals with basic rituals. Set aside caste, religion, etc. The departing soul deserves that last respects to be paid to the mortal remains. Instead of dumping bodies in a pit or consigning them to fire, an appropriate burial with prayers is what I intend to give them".

Sreedhar decided on making this his mission with the support of Vishranthi in the initial years. As soon as he hears about a death, he would seek permission to take leave from his regular work place and perform the final rites, and then return to work.

Setting up a trust: After a few years, he started the 'Anatha Pretha Kainkarya Trust' (APKT). He felt that if he were to extend his services further, he needed to have a more formal approach, especially since handling unclaimed bodies required support. A few other people from different walks of life joined him in his service. To enable him to proceed further with his plans, he then tied up with well-known NGOs like SaiCharan, Aanandam, Kaakkum Karangal, Nimmadhi, Premalaya, and some homes for war widows and the mentally challenged. Some of these institutions were orphanages, and in such cases, the last rites were performed in a way consistent with the religion of the deceased.

The biggest challenge lay in burial of unclaimed bodies in mortuaries. They bury unclaimed dead bodies after lengthy police procedures and clearance. Sreedhar mostly gets call from hospitals at indefinite time spans indicating a specific time plan for disposal. The most likely days are Sundays.

Teamwork: He now has the support of volunteers supporting him from different walks of life, like a retired senior police official, young employees from IT companies and private firms. This author was touched when he had occasion to note that women too had become part of this service. This statement is not intended to reflect a gender bias but none can discount the hold of unbroken social beliefs that does not approve of woman visiting burial ground. Modern liberal attitudes have resulted in gradual erosion of such beliefs. When questioned, one of the women volunteers said she was there as she was a young widow and derived emotional satisfaction from participating in this service. One must appreciate the courage and spirit behind this act of defying tradition and coming to fight human predicament even after cessation of life.

It is important to note that it is not an easy environment to provide service. Sreedhar and his volunteers fight against several odds in disposing of the dead in a decent manner and in keeping with customary rituals. Often, mortuaries impose severe limitations resulting from constrained resources. Legal and other delays often lead to severe decomposition of bodies. Staff may have work-related issues that may reflect adversely in their performance.

Sreedhar is considerate and appreciative of the staff and workers at mortuaries, crematoriums and burial grounds. The public does not comprehend the occupational hazards they face, and thus, people who visit these places—usually under some compulsion—do not cooperate with the staff all the way. Sometimes, when they do mass burials, earth excavators may not be available for some reason or the other. These are realities they have to put up with.

Sreedhar recalls that one cannot expect a warm reception from society when one works on arranging funerals for unclaimed bodies. He strongly feels that all volunteers must be humble and willing to work through all odds. Sometimes, a simple down to earth approach is required to resolve issues. He cited an example. One particular day during the monsoon, his team had carried a large number of bodies from a mortuary in a van. Typically, the schedule calls for all of them to assemble at the mortuary around 8 a.m., handle the formalities and leave in a van with the bodies received by 10 a.m. Once the burial ground is reached, Sreedhar is joined by his volunteers. The dead, where their faith is identifiable get a funeral according to the faith they practiced. In other cases, volunteer Odhuvars begin reciting the Siva Puranam with total devotion befitting the occasion for about an hour. Mr. Arokiaraj a volunteer now gives a Christian prayer committing the soul to the Lord God. Then the corpses get lowered, with all outward purification done and dressed up and covered with shroud, into the pit. After the pit is covered with earth, the team of volunteers sings in chorus 'Ragu pathi Raghava Raja Ram'. Listening to Sreedhar, one would conclude that it is worth dying to deserve this kind of a finale. The funeral given stands in sharp contrast to several unemotional send-offs given by relatives, who perform, uninvolved, as though they are completing a painful duty. The team would typically complete the last rites by noon, when members would return to their respective homes.

On that particular day, they reached the mortuary at around 11 a.m. An excavator was required at the burial ground as there were 30 bodies. An excavator was arranged from elsewhere as the one regularly used in that ground failed. But the two staff members at the burial ground were running fever and could not do any work. Digging pits for corpses is not an activity that one can plan out in advance, especially during monsoon. At about 3 p.m., they decided that they would have to dig the pit themselves, as it was not appropriate to keep the bodies out for long. While they were digging, their van had to leave, and they worked at getting the bodies out. Sreedhar recalled that not only was his team handling the labor comfortably, but also the ground staff members, without heed to their illness, were helping in a spirited manner. Leaders need to demonstrate their skills by keeping workers together and Sreedhar excels in doing that.

It bears mentioning here that Sreedhar recently retired from the post of Vice President—Operations of a large, well-known financial services company. One of his friends informed this author that there were occasions when Sreedhar would take his coat off and leave the office, finish the last rites of a corpse or more and come right back to work. Sreedhar demonstrates commitment to the cause and the desire to live by practicing what he believes. Over the last three decades Sreedhar has performed the last rites for 1,430 persons with solemnity.

Funding: Each cremation costs between Rs. 1,000 and 1,500. APKT manages these expenses from its funds. During the initial days, Sreedhar used his personal money on several occasions.

There was one touching experience he had while doing this. A woman who had an income of barely Rs. 12 a day contributed one day's earning to him. She was a stranger, and he had not sought funds from her. She volunteered on hearing about his services from neighborhood sources. Sreedhar feels that funding would never be an issue for him in extending this service.

Other Sevarthis (service providers): Sreedhar mentioned to this author that many other people offer the same service as he does. A lady by name Neila, has been burying dead bodies from government hospital for a decade along with her two sons. Trivikrama Mahadeva in Bangalore has been doing this for more than four decades. A flower vendor in Coimbatore, Shanta Kumar, is reportedly doing the same thing, and so are Umar Ali and his friends at Udamalpet. Reports also state that the Chennai-based advocate Venkatasubramaniam's 'Jeevatma Kainkaryam Trust' offers these services while Raghavan, a retired Chennai Telephones employee, offers his Chromepet Gayathri Trust's services depending upon need.

All such good work needs to be commended and supported. Some of the people involved in this kind of work have been recognized by governments and towering personalities. The point here is that Sreedhar is one among the few who undertake these distinctly humane activities. What is common to all of them is the trigger that caused them to turn inwards, and carry out socially significant work with humility, focus and in utter disregard of care returns. Nishkamya seva or service unmindful of returns cannot go beyond. A good cause attracts team support and strength for execution.

Family involvement: Sreedhar's family has demonstrated this spirit. His grandfather listened to Paramacharya's father who was an Inspector of Schools in the early years of 19th century. The sage's father advised Sreedhar's grandfather to start a primary school in their native village. Paying heed to the advice the family set up a primary school which has rendered several decades of service and is going strong now, under a different management. As Sreedhar grew up, serving fellow humans became his desire, but he wanted to do so alongside providing for his family's needs by working. He did good and gainful employment and went on to become a Vice President of a financial company. After the initial years of service, the demand on his time and energies began to increase and he started allotting more time mainly to his social activity and to a lesser extent to his family. His wife extends her unstinted support, and more surprisingly, encourages her children to join their father in his service. His elder son is an active member of his team. His younger son lives abroad but participates whenever he comes to India. According to Sreedhar, it is critical to get family understanding and support for such activities.

Conclusion: Sreedhar has more dreams, like assisting severe cancer patients, renovation of old temples. The Kanchi seer's writing influenced him to take up the odd service of burial arrangement with a sense of pride and the desire to pay due last respects to those who otherwise remain unclaimed. This kind of meaningful engagement can co-exist with the normal passions for building a career and sustaining a family, when one has an understanding spouse and supportive children. If more people like Sreedhar were to extend their hands, this world of the living would become a better place by giving peace to the dead.

CHAPTER 6

Little drops make an ocean:
Jayanthi Ramesh, Founder, Maitri Trust

Introduction: Some conventional professionals are highly educated and are able to find employment in multinational companies early in life. They may also have done well in their career progression. Others found exceptional opportunities working in cozy jobs in the Middle East for the best of the world's brands. Just imagine somebody in such a position, who suddenly faced family pressure to relocate back to India with family, so that the children could be given quality education and absorb family traditions and native social and cultural facets like dance and music. Normally such a person could easily relocate to another IT job in India, especially if that person is an early-stage qualifier for Project Management Professional certification!

This chapter discusses a person who could do all of this but decided to do something else. If you consider the face value of the actions of this person, they may not be astounding. However, if you could realize the spirit behind those actions, you would be stunned. The path Jayanthi

Ramesh chose to follow was to impact children in her neighborhood. Let us understand the trigger and challenges that sent her down this path.

Early days: Jayanthi was born in a conservative, high-class family to parents who believed in ensuring she imbibed the right values and spirits from childhood. Her father worked at Dalmia Cements in Dalmiapuram (also called Kallakudi), which is about 42 km from Trichy. He lived with his family in a residential campus that was pretty much a cosmopolitan society, as the personnel and their families were from all parts of the country. Jayanthi grew up learning and understanding the philanthropy of Y.H. Dalmia through the projects he sponsored. These projects were focused on Dalmiapuram and its surrounding areas, as well as in UP and Eastern India, where the Dalmia group had a strong base.

Under the leadership of N. Gopalaswamy, the then General Manager of Dalmia Cements, the company used to organize various activities. These activities include sports at the national and state levels; religious discourses by veterans such as Pulavar Keeran and Kirupanandha Variyar; musical performances by great singers including the world famous M.S. Subbulakshmi; *bhajans*; debates on Tamil literary values by stalwarts; various dramas and skits with moral messages performed by stalwarts such as Manohar and Cho. Ramaswamy. This type of a 'positive' environment served not only the purpose of recreation but also as seeds of personality development.

As she was in school, Jayanthi read the works of Mother Teresa. She was deeply touched by these humble works. She strongly felt that the characteristics described in those works needed to be imbibed by anyone who wants to serve his or her fellow humans. Even in her younger age, Jayanthi was influenced by the following quote of Mother Teresa: "Not all of us can do great things. But we can do small things with great love".

Apart from being influenced by Mother Teresa's work, Jayanthi was also influenced by her parents in practising humility in conduct towards society. Her father was a soft-spoken man who introduced her to philosophy. Her mother was the embodiment of service in her own way. She used to keep buttermilk during the summer in a vessel outside her home for public consumption, and never bothered to find out who availed of the soothing liquid. She believed that it would quench the thirst of the needy. For her, it was immaterial who exactly the needy were. In the same way, she used to distribute food to people in and around her neighborhood irrespective of considerations like religion or caste. She arranged free tuition for poor children, and further, encouraged them to sing and dance. These activities were not to help her pass time, but were the result of a passion to make people around her happy, healthy and vibrant.

Jayanthi was so highly influenced by her parents that she wanted to take up social work. She studied IT in a college in Trichy and did very well. Immediately after her studies, she got married to Ramesh, who took her to the Middle East after a few months. She worked for 14 years in the IT field, including 8 years with a leading airline in the UAE.

Trigger: Jayanthi loves reading books, especially those by Dr. Abdul Kalam. His vision for India 2020 appealed to her. His positive statements on the scope for each individual to contribute to a 'Developed India' impressed her greatly. Reading Paramacharya's writing titled "Deviathin Kural" influenced Jayanthi further. As mentioned earlier, there came a time when Jayanthi decided to move to Chennai to groom her children. She had domestic help at home. One day, her domestic help naively asked her if her children could also study with Jayanthi's kids and thus get some support for their academic efforts. Jayanthi was thrilled, and asked the help's children to come to her home regularly for study. In fact, she spent more time with the help's two kids, who were in standards eight and six. Though she found some improvement, she was not happy with their progress. The unsatisfied Jayanthi probed further and found out that she had started supporting them rather late, and hence, they were finding it difficult to catch up.

Instead of going back to work for an IT company, she decided to dedicate her time to teaching poor children. During her daily walks, she used to see an *anganwadi* centre near her residence. *Anganwadis* are centres run by the Integrated Child Development Services that provide day care to children in the age group 2-6 when their poor parents are out at work. The *anganwadi* program is government-supported. Most people would assume that these *anganwadis* were not very exciting to associate with for someone like Jayanthi. However, she made a decision in the exact opposite direction and started to work with the *anganwadis*, propelled by her passion to provide education for young children.

Challenges: Jayanthi's first challenge was, of course, to decide on the role/capacity to adopt when working with *anganwadis*. If she were to engage with *anganwadis*, she could not do so as an individual. She needed to be part of a formal social welfare set up, or start a trust by herself. Since she was not familiar with the validation processes involved in association with the right kind of NGO, she decided to give up that option. If she had to register a trust, she had to go through bureaucratic processes for which she required help from a legal expert and a chartered accountant. She went through this process and registered "Maitritrust". She took the help of some seniors in social service who had gone through this process.

To teach at *anganwadis*, Jayanthi required training in the Montessori Method of teaching. Any other pedagogy was not likely to work as well in enabling her to be effective to the maximum extent. She had to invest in material for teaching. As she started working with *anganwadis*, demands on her time increased. She started finding it difficult to spare enough time to be effective in a few demanding *anganwadis*. She recruited Montessori-trained teachers to support her cause.

In spite of the support from the government in granting the necessary approvals and the wonderful grasp of the *anganwadi* children, the primary challenge continued to be motivating the *anganwadi* workers and helpers to do their jobs in a child-friendly manner. In order to resolve this problem, Jayanthi conducted training on Montessori methodology and basic soft skills for the workers and helpers of 20 *anganwadis*. She later mentioned that the success rate of 50% gave her the motivation to conduct further training workshops.

Add on services: Jayanthi felt the need to move further ahead, to educating children of higher grades. She visited nearby corporation-run schools and offered her time to conduct value-added courses on topics such as soft skills, value education, environmental awareness, personal health and hygiene and creativity. Though she knew that she could not do all this by herself, she did not have the money to employ field workers who could deliver these services.

She networked with some likeminded women who could spare a few hours every week. She connected them with the corporation schools. Now she is able to take nearly 23 classes in six different schools. She focuses on helping students to gain higher education so that they are enabled to move on to university education and then make appropriate career choices.

Though funding continues to be a serious challenge that hinders her from upscaling as she would like to, she is still able to deliver an appreciate level of service with the right kind of associations, donors and resource providers like those who give their time free of cost. She is not interested in promoting her trust from the fund-raising perspective, as she believes that she must maintain her own ambit of control to enable her to do things well and in a meaningful way. She is not keen to be known outside her circle for her work, as she feels it to be nothing more her own, personal way of creating value.

Family: Jayanthi's parents gave her lot of encouragement right from her adolescence to explore whatever she wanted to achieve in social service. They taught her the values of humility and an unselfish approach towards service. They also taught her to do what is manageable and clearly measurable as a way of service. After her marriage, her husband and her mother-in-law also encouraged her to pursue her passion to serve her fellow humans, building on her own areas of strength. She is blessed with two children, both of them enjoy their mother's involvement in social service. Though born in the supposedly higher social echelon in this part of India, Jayanthi loves working with *anganwadi* children, who long for love and affection. For Jayanthi, this is like serving a higher, divine power, as all of us are children of God!

Conclusion: Jayanthi may be doing simple social service in a limited way. However, she believes these are nothing but simple efforts that many others could also quietly make. Such efforts would succeed in bringing about revolutionary social change in India. As seen in this approach, it may not be important to rely solely on government policies and systems to take care of the poor and the underprivileged. Jayanthi believes that each one of us is obliged to make society healthy and vibrant by donating our time and intellect to uplift our fellow humans. Helping children with education is the best thing to do, as this is what that takes them forward to becoming better citizens. If only the beliefs and values of Jayanthi were more prevalent, we would be seeing substantive qualitative improvements in the world around us.

CHAPTER 7

Age is inconsequential for impacting a change: Padmini Gopalan, Sri Ramacharan Charitable Trust

Introduction: The author comes from a suburban town in Tamil Nadu that is significantly influenced by some important historical and social factors. First, the town had a significant British presence in the days when they ruled India. This led to the adoption of a formal working style that was followed from Monday to Friday. More importantly, it led to planned lifestyles and retirement at a certain age, to enable better quality of life. Second, the town is surrounded by an agrarian society of people who believe in working hard during their active life spans before passing over the baton of leadership and hard work to the next generation. The elderly generation settles for respect and a retired life. Third, the town was ruled by Dravidian monarchs for a large part of its history. It was the capital of a ruling dynasty for a substantial period, when a number of temples were built. The influence of the system, such that people are groomed to respect their elders, survives to this day. Elders pass on their active work lives to the next generation and become socially active at some point during their advancing years. Of course, these are good qualities virtues, except that elders think armchairs are a preferable option to going out to drive beneficial change in society.

This attitude is also prevalent in many other parts of India, where people believe retirement is the normal conclusion to their vocational life and plan for it. Exceptions arise only in politics, where the word retirement is taboo.

Against this backdrop, we talk about a lady who, at 72 years of age, decides to work for the good of poor children in her own way. We discuss Padmini Gopalan's efforts, triggers and challenges.

Background: Padmini was a member of the Monday Charity Club, which was started by the famous Savithri Vaithi (Exhibit 1), a gerontologist who runs Vishranthi, a home for destitute women on Chennai's East Coast Road. Vishranthi came up when someone mooted the idea of an old age home at one of the Monday Charity Club's meetings. Padmini was associated with the old age home.

About a decade back, four of her friends decided to do something for children. Padmini was deeply concerned by the lack of infrastructure and committed staff at schools, especially those that are run by local governments through municipality corporations. Padmini mentioned that people generally find private schools more attractive. The question that then arose was: how many people can afford to send their children to private schools? Those who cannot afford private schools compromise on the quality of the education their children get. Determined to do something about this situation, she initiated action to impact children studying in corporation schools.

Exhibit 1—A champion of an old age destitute home in Chennai

Savithri Vaithi, born in Salem, was said to have initially had a comfortable childhood. She was forced to give up schooling when her family fell on hard times. Her first job was in a social welfare centre that took care of children and women. She learnt about the challenges of life faced by the deprived there. After her marriage in 1954, she stared teaching them fine arts and other means for empowerment. Together with other like-minded people, she formed the Monday Charity Club as well.

Savithiri started Vishranthi in 1978. This caters to older destitute women, because the poor suffer more as they grow old. The Trust was launched in Chrompet in a rented home before it moved to the East Coast Road. Today, it has 150 elderly members, 30 staff and 10 helpers.

Vishranthi has separate blocks for the old, the bedridden, and the mentally challenged, besides a nursing home for emergencies and a small orphanage.

Savithri has authored many books on old age, including a directory of old-age homes and a guide to starting and maintaining an old-age home. Among the various awards she has received are: the Jawaharlal Nehru Award and the Melwin Jones Worthy Fellow Award.

She has effected some remarkable changes, often contrary to tradition, in the status of women, like encouraging them to light the funeral pyres of their relatives under compelling circumstances. Though Savithiri is 82 years old, she refuses to allow her age to impose limits on her activities; she still works full time on the old age home's activities.

Source: Age cannot wither her, Anusha Parthasarathy, The Hindu, August 23, 2013. http://www.thehindu.com/features/the-yin-thing/age-cannot-wither-her/article5055881.ece

---

Opportunities and challenges: Padmini went to a corporation-run school near her home to provide free tuitions to students with the help of other teachers. She thought that she would be welcome. She found the system inadequate and the children underprepared. It was a revelation for her to find out that the children were not comfortably able to write even the basic alphabets. She decided to start teaching the lower classes of students, as they were more receptive to absorbing and learning things. However, she faced problems with the administration. Quite a few administrators were cynical about her involvement in a government set-up. One of the corporation-run schools challenged her to take the place of a class four teacher who was on a long leave. Without a teacher, the children from that class were running all over the school during school time, disturbing all other classes. Padmini took up the challenge in all seriousness.

She approached a famous lawyer, who in his wisdom advised Padmini that it could be appropriate to accept the challenge and take up the role at the school, but cautioned that it was not a common occurrence, and possibly was not wise, either. Padmini was worried about issues like reporting relationships, hierarchies and the administration. She had been working with an agency called Child Vikas International, based in the USA. When the president of that agency was on one of his regular visits to India, he went to the school where Padmini wanted to initiate action. He was impressed with the idea but was worried about how Padmini could effectively work with the government.

The uncertainty ended when a proactive administrator who fortuitously visited the school asked her to go ahead with her idea, commenting, "Good ideas must have concrete suggestions of overwhelming opportunities rather than looking through a constrained window of gloom". This gave her the first breakthrough.

Within three months, the school was requesting her to take over kindergarten classes, as two teachers went on maternity leave. Padmini was excited by the idea and contacted a few of her friends to gain an understanding of the scope for introducing the Montessori Method of learning to these classes. This attracted severe criticism that corporation-run schools and children who are from low-income groups may not be the ideal choice for such a system of learning.

Padmini decided to probe the workings of the Montessori system further, as she had never personally been involved with such a system. All that she knew was that it was more of experiential learning. She approached Uma Shanker, the Director at the Centre for Montessori

Training, Chennai. Uma encouraged Padmini and recommended two teachers who Padmini could appoint for the corporation-run school.

These teachers were dedicated, and after having a look at the school, they got excited. They gave Padmini a list of material to procure before the start of the sessions, including things like mats, cutting boards, knives and toys. Padmini wondered about the feasibility of going ahead, but invested Rs. 60,000 for the purchases. After a week, she got a call from the school complaining about the two teachers, who, instead of teaching the children the alphabet, were making them cut carrots and other vegetables and freeing them from their classrooms, allowing them to do what they wanted.

Padmini reiterated her confidence that the two teachers would bring about a positive change in culture. After three months, the teachers invited her to meet the children. What she saw was miraculous!

Change elements: The children were well groomed. They were neat and clean. They were wearing freshly washed clothes. They were excited about coming to school, something acknowledged by their parents. Though they were in the 3-4 age range, they were adept at cutting vegetables, and were proud of being able to do so. The lesson taught to them was to do everything with concentration and do it whenever they wanted. They were excited. The children were united and sharing. They were helping each other, and recognizing and participating in one another's activities.

Their discipline was exemplary. They used mats for sitting on when working. When done, they folded the mats by themselves. Their parents reported to Padmini that they were demonstrating the same discipline at home as well. This was real, lasting learning, rather than the kind of learning that involved studying for examinations and forgetting the lessons soon after. In all probability, the latter kind of learning was what the traditional system was providing them, even at the higher academic grades.

Padmini felt that her decision to go ahead with the Montessori Method of learning had been right, as she felt it was "too good instead of challenging". She knew that going ahead with conviction in implementing a system you believe in is what leadership is all about.

She observed that the children in the age group three to six were confident and bold. They could look into her eyes and express themselves on what and how they felt about something. The author feels that such traits are missing even at higher education levels in so-called centres of excellence or at work, where people choose to speak what their teachers or bosses would like to hear.

Padmini strongly believes that instead of systematically eroding self-esteem, the Montessori Method of learning instills the confidence to speak out what is right. Having a generation of people looking into your eyes and speaking their minds is what society needs today. Padmini believes this is achievable in any strata of society and need not be the prerogative of high-end private schools and their administrations. She was taken aback when in three months the children transformed from a group criticized for running around disturbing everyone to a group "commanding respect".

The change was observed by the school administration and the local government as well. The corporation commissioner visited the school and congratulated Padmini; he asked her to take over more schools.

She took on a few more schools, but politely explained that scalability was not her strength. The commissioner saw the point, and then an interesting thing happened.

The Chennai Corporation adopted the Montessori Learning Method as the standard and trained their teachers to implement the method in all schools with kindergarten classes. Thus, came about the success of Padmini's experiment and intervention. It may be worth noting that even Mahatma Gandhi had appreciated the Montessori Method of Learning.

Involvement in Balwadis: Balwadi schools provide pre-school education to children in the age group 3-5. They are run in urban areas where children from low-income families do not have access to the *anganwadi* centres run by the government or to any other pre-school facility run by the private sector, including other NGOs (http://www.balwadi.org.in/).

Padmini, who has about 30 teachers under her wing, decided to get associated with a few Balwadis centres in the Mylapore and Saidapet areas of Chennai. Teachers use the Montessori Method with high impact. Padmini closely monitors their activities. She regularly discusses the progress of the children with their parents. The parents report to her that the children are eager to go to their Balwadi centres, and look forward to each day of interaction. The centres work around the year, and though Padmini grants teachers holidays in rotation, both children and teachers are happy to meet every day and continue with experiential learning. A file is maintained for every child, with constant updates on his or her progress.

Some of the interesting observations are:

1. Children quickly learn the habits of cleanliness and discipline and try to instill them at home. Mothers particularly are very happy about such children, who bring in a degree of social pride for the family.

2. On observation, it was found that as these children progress to primary schools, they impact those schools by bringing about positive change. They demonstrate leadership in simple ways. For example, when a new student enrolls in a school, the other children trained at Balwadi guide newly admitted students to a seat and share what they can to make their newly joined mates feel comfortable.

3. Sibling care is emphasized, as elder children who have gone on from Balwadi to primary schools monitor the younger ones who remain in Balwadi schools.

These pleasant results give Padmini a sense of satisfaction and further motivate her to continue driving this change.

Family background: Padmini is of the opinion that to achieve such wonderful changes, family support is essential. However, she advises those who want to get involved in social work to first balance their family responsibilities and social endeavors in the right mix. She feels that as long as people face up to family responsibilities with discipline, they will never find it difficult to undertake social work.

In fact, she proudly says that her daughter, who is a doctor, encourages her to continue with social work, as it keeps Padmini fit and agile. It is important to have a clear mindset, defined goals and an action plan to take up the right activities. She feels that for any person to be a successful reformist, two things are essential: humility and the habit of practicing what the person preaches. For example, Padmini is a simple and humble person. She has sharp opinions on vulgar expressions of elitism. She feels that such expressions are what offend fellow humans and create imbalanced relationships. The ability to treat people with respect and human in whatever they do is what brings about positive change. Padmini feels these traits must be practiced at home first.

Conclusion: Padmini's work could be inconsequential to many who do not understand the bottom of our social pyramid. She has demonstrated the need for change its ability to impact. Local governments have accepted this necessity. She is a mentor and motivator for many who follow her footsteps. Children revere her a lot, and this may flourish further in future as they grow up. Her activities are not an individual's way of passing time meaningfully but reflect a craving for bring about positive change in society. If only more of us think in the same way as Padmini, that is, that taking action can actually influence social change, we could work miracles for the world around us. It is not just machines that need *kaizen* (continuous improvement), society does, too!

CHAPTER 8

Partnering for social cause:
Shaikh Vazir E, Promoter, Textile unit, Tiruppur

Introduction: One often hears stories of migrants from rural India making efforts to achieve a dignified living in the metros and large urban conglomerates of India. In particular, metros like Mumbai, Delhi, Kolkata, Chennai and Bangalore have many people from other states. They live under tough conditions, because they need to focus on making both ends meet. They find comfort within their own newly formed groups. Their children grow up and pursue lifestyle aspirations that are more ambitious. Generally, the next generation of all migrants focuses more on going up the financial and social ladders. It becomes a major, welcome change when they move from a small house to a single bedroom home. They struggle to progress, because life is just as competitive for the second generation as for the first. The struggle is tougher on fair, ethical and honest people who do not believe in short cuts to success or in working to earn quick bucks. A large part of the labor force in urban India comes from such backgrounds. They constitute a vital resource pool and directly contribute to the growth of India.

Here, we talk about Vazir, who had a humble, if not deprived, background. He went to become an entrepreneur. Let us study how he worked with partner within his ecosystem to give back to society by supporting a kids' school and furthering the higher education of a selected few children.

Early days: Vazir was born to a traditional family in Brahmavara, a village near Udipi in one of the South Canara districts. He was the youngest among three brothers. His father was a tailor. Traditionally, most of the workforce from South Canara has moved abroad, especially to the gulf countries, to earn a higher income. However, Vazir's father decided to move to Mumbai. He was highly patriotic and felt that the Indian soil provided equal opportunities to all those who are committed to the motherland. Vazir's father, his immediate brother and he moved to Mumbai. They lived in a small house at Khar (East). His father set up a tailoring shop and employed a couple of locals to facilitate him in running the shop.

Vazir and his brother studied at a Kannada Association-run school at Bandra, as it was affordable. However, they had to commute a considerable distance every day to attend school. Vazir was ambitious and was studious. He completed his graduation in commerce and then pursued law.

Changing fortunes: This was when a leading domestic soft drink brand that was growing aggressively offered a job as salesman to Vazir. He discontinued his BGL law course to join this company. It was his bad luck that the company had labor problems, and he was jobless soon.

It looked like his decision to discontinue his education was wrong. He decided to fight back.

He worked at different jobs in a printing press, the PWD department and a hotel. It was while he was working as a receptionist in a hotel that his life took a major turn.

By nature, Vazir was extrovert and was used to helping people. He had frequent interactions with European buyers of garments who stayed at the hotel. Because of his discussions with them, he developed a keen interest in the garments industry. He decided to look for opportunities to learn more about the trade.

By this time, his family, which had prospered a little, had moved to a larger single bedroom flat at Santa Cruz. With his father, Vazir discussed the information he had obtained from the garment buyers he met at the hotel. He developed a sound understanding of the processes involved in the manufacture of garments and in buying and exporting them.

Vazir decided on a "high risk high return" approach to business, instead of staying content with marginal growth and a secured life. However, he felt that he was still not ready, and decided to work in a garments factory that has substantial exports. He got a job to work as executive assistant to a promoter of a large export house that was doing around Rs. 100 cores of business then. In three years, Vazir learnt most of the nuances of the trade and grew fast in his job. The promoter was extremely happy with him, as Vazir understood buyers' needs and excelled at maintaining the kind of sound relationship that furthered the business.

Loyal to the core: Vazir believed loyalty as a core value and in hard work as a way of life. The promoter gave him a loan to buy his own flat, making him hopeful of leading a comfortable life in Mumbai. The promoter bought him a first class train pass, considered a status symbol among professionals in Mumbai those days. Vazir was a young bachelor and all these amounted to multiple achievements for him.

At this point, something significant happened in his life. It is important to note here that buyers from abroad used to buy garments from trading houses in Mumbai and Delhi that were made in Tiruppur,

Ludhiana and other industrial belts of India. This system existed mainly because in those days, trading houses had a flair for trading, while manufacturers generally lacked that tact. This was a convention driven by cultural differences and other aspects of social inequality. Language was another important barrier, as many of the locals could not speak in any language other than their vernacular.

The previous two decades had seen a phenomenal growth in the trade of garments from Tiruppur (Exhibit 1). A number of foreign buyers were exploring the possibilities for opening their own offices in Coimbatore, Bangalore or Tiruppur to cut out intermediaries in the supply chain. They needed a local person from the region to represent their interests.

One buyer from Switzerland, impressed by Vazir's zeal, offered him a job. Vazir was to set up an office in Tiruppur for the buyer and directly handle buying volumes for exports. Though it looked like a dream opportunity for Vazir, he declined, stating that his employer was generous and that taking up the offer would constitute a clear conflict of interest. The buyer suggested that the trading house could continue to handle the order management with Vazir at Tiruppur for quality control. At a later state, they could consider evaluating a more direct relationship. Again, Vazir declined that the suggestion jade for a convenience-based arrangement that still infringed on his loyalty to his promoter. Vazir told the buyer he would be accept the offer if the promoter also approved of such an arrangement, a circumstance which did not arise. The buyer left his contact details with Vazir and asked him to connect whenever he was ready to re-evaluate the proposal.

Dramatic change of events: About two decades back, a dramatic series of events worked out in favor of Vazir. Ongoing social unrest and communal disturbances disrupted the lives of Vazir and his family. Though his promoter was helpful, Vazir felt that the pressures on his family were too high. Suddenly, Vazir and his family were reduced to having nothing. Fear of the future engulfed them.

Vazir had informed his promoter about the opportunity given to him by the buyer from Switzerland. He had asked for the promoter's views, as

Vazir felt the need to go independent to achieve his growth aspirations would arise at some point in time. Vazir thought that this juncture, when he was facing an uncertain future, could be the right time to put into action his ambition for pursuing growth elsewhere.

The promoter gladly welcomed the idea, but on the condition that Vazir would not be appraising his products on behalf of the buyer. The dilemma could be resolved only if Vazir could take over the buyer's business and solicit new suppliers. It was a challenge for the buyer, who had had a long relationship with the promoter's company, and critical for that company, as it would lose a significant volume of business, and thereby, profits. By what you could call the work of the hand of god or chance, both the buyer and the promoter decided to sail with Vazir. In fact, the promoter released Vazir's home loan document in a day to expedite his move to Tiruppur.

Vazir came to Tiruppur to set up an office for the Swiss buyer. He did not know Tamil, the local language of Tiruppur, and he had no friends in the town. He did not have a place yet, nor did he have transport. He had just been married. Sheer grit made him move to Tiruppur. In spite of these obstacles, Vazir progressed, thanks to the opportunities the town and its trade potential offered. In a matter of a few years, he had promoted his own company with the blessings of the buyer, becoming an independent manufacturer and directly handling export orders to clients including that first Swiss buyer. This progress reflected the spirit of entrepreneurism in him.

Giving it back to society: Vazir felt that his growth from being a nobody to becoming a successful independent businessman was due to the following factors:

1. his drive and hard work even in trying circumstances
2. his values and belief in the virtues of honesty, openness and transparency
3. most importantly, the trust and opportunity his employers gave him and his own ability to maintain both loyalty and individuality

4. the spirit of Tiruppur town and the ability to ride on a wave of growth in the industry.

He brought his parents, his brothers and their families to Tiruppur and helped them to settle down comfortably. Some time ago, a trust running a kindergarten school near Tiruppur had sought financial help from him. He had been giving money every year to that trust, which was run with the support of a lady from Switzerland by a local person named Mahesh. Suddenly, Mahesh died. The Swiss lady could not run the trust and was looking out for local partners.

At this point, Vazir and Nicolas, a buyer (a key supply chain player in business) from abroad who procured material to order from Vazir, joined hands in taking up the opportunity. They promised to support the trust. Vazir now runs the school, which has 40 children. Nicolas and his friends support the initiative.

It is worth noting the level of mutual understanding and trust Nicolas and Vazir had. While they shared business interests and were able to discuss issues in a fair and transparent manner, their relationship went beyond business to do something socially good for the geography from where procurement took place. Their joint success substantiates their ability to offer value not only for their immediate stakeholders, but also to create value for the society they lived in through their mutual partnership. In fact, Nicolas had been handling similar work at Thailand. The degree of harmony between him and Vazir, for whom he is a procurer, is phenomenal.

His support may look small at a casual glance, but the impact is meaningful. Every year, they sponsor two boys and two girls at a school in Avinashi. These children receive all support until they complete their education.

The system works like this. A foreigner emotionally and financially adopts each child and sponsors his or her education. The adopter funds all necessities like books and other accessories and school fees. All of the children have done well in their studies. Over the years, the first batch of students has reached the seventh grade. The system runs smoothly. The trust gives complete details and access to the donors.

The donors visit the school regularly. They celebrate Deepavali, Christmas, New Year and Pongal. The key buyer and supporter of this program, Nicholas, participates in all activities.

You should note the depth of the partnership Vazir established with his buyer to set up social initiatives and run them successfully. The two of them are hopeful of making this a sustainable initiative by funding as many children as possible.

All the financial support is routed and handled through a legal structure. The trust that Vazir runs has his family and friends from India as trustees. They can take financial support as it comes and file necessary documents. In fact, Vazir, Nicolas and their friends have plans of taking this activity, "Take Care Kids—India", into a large organization over the years and attain a stage when an orphanage can be built. He feels this is the best way to give back to society. Incidentally, it will also establish the best standards of "Responsible Procurement Programme" which Europeans passionately talk about when they participate in social programs.

Conclusion: Vazir feels that those who were benevolent to him were human and agonistic about social factors. And in the same manner Vazir wants to fashion his "giving" and his highly human approach to impacting the needy and helping them realize their dreams. It may be difficult to believe, but Vazir personally spends time on each child's selection and progress and personally reports to donors so that they can see the impact. Today, he feels sorry that he could fund only four students out of the initial, fully funded batch of 40. However, he is convinced that the rest of the 36 are also progressing well, as other benevolent people continue to support these children. As this author said in the case of another champion, it is not just operational size that matters, it is the intent, impact and a genuine approach that motivate many others to do something useful to society. As the cycle spreads out, more projects come up, and most of them would also scale up. What society needs is more people like Vazir who enjoy "giving back" to society and are true champions of social responsibility. There is no law that compels him to do this. There are consultants who suggest that time spent on social work can be charged in monetary terms using normal cost factors. However, that approach ignores the huge difference that would be made to the world if we have many more people, like Vazir, who volunteer to impact society through positive change!

Exhibit 1. Tiruppur Exports

Exports from Tiruppur grew from a meager Rs. 10 crores in 1985 to 5,000 crores in 2003 and to 11,000 crores in 2006-2007. This performance has no parallel anywhere in the world.

The following table captures the yearly export data from Tiruppur between 1985 and 2009.

YEAR-WISE EXPORT DATA

YEAR	QUANTITY (Lakh Pieces)	Value (Rs. Crores)	YEAR	QUANTITY (Lakh Pieces)	Value (Rs. Crores)
1984	104.2	9.69	1997	2,983	2,255
1985	172.1	18.69	1998	3,461	2,619
1986	288.7	37.48	1999	3,764	3,067
1987	333.56	74.49	2000	4,243	3,581
1988	459.06	104.24	2001	3,831	3,528
1989	614	167.39	2002	3,580	3,250
1990	888.73	289.85	2003	3,812	3,896
1991	905.11	429.48	2004	4,114	4,468.8
1992	1,399	774.93	2004-05		6,500
1993	1,893	1162.4	2005-06		8,500
1994	1,964	1318	2006-07		11,000
1995	2,171	1591.8	2007-08		9,950
1996	2,574	1897	2008-09		5,050
			(April-Sept.)		

Leading brands such as Nike, Cutter & Buck, Adidas, GAP, Tommy Hilfiger, Katzenberg, Van Heusen, Fila and Arrow and leading chain stores like C&A, Wal-Mart, Target, Sears, Mothers Care and H&M are sourcing from Tiruppur. In fact, one of the garment manufacturers in Tiruppur supplied T-shirts to the FIFA World Cup.

Due to the impact of adverse external factors like the appreciation of the rupee against the US dollar, the financial crises in the US and EU markets and the rise in petro-product prices and bank interest rates, there the targets for 2012 were not realized.

Source: http://tiruppur.nic.in/textile.html

CHAPTER 9

Serving tribal children:
Dr. C Satheesh Kumar, Ekal Vidyalaya

Introduction: In Kanyakumari, in a border district down in South India, people are known for their hard work and commitment to fulfilling their dreams. The general tendency for a typical middle-class family would be to educate the children and instill in them the values of the service class. Dr. C. Satheesh Kumar, who was born in Nagarkoil, has taken to a different path, social service. In this chapter, we discuss how he looked up various career options and finally committed himself to making a positive impact on society through his deeds. This decision arose out of a passion, in existence from childhood, to improve the lives of fellow humans. Converting such decisions into action means sacrifice and asks for unquestionable devotion, humility and selflessness.

Early days: Satheesh was born to a middle class, conservative family. His father was a lorry driver and his mother was a homemaker. He studied in a government school. He took a lot of interest in moral science classes, and was fond of inspiring stories. He also attended Vellai Vallai Ashram classes and Bala Kendra, and drew inspiration from lectures he heard, when very young, on serving the nation. The seeds of social service were sown in those days, when he hardly understood what it meant to translate dreams into action.

After completing his secondary school education, Satheesh registered for a course on Ayurveda (BAMS) at a college in Coimbatore. This is a well-known institution that produces a number of ayurvedic doctors who practice alternate medical services based on herbs and natural sources. Satheesh is of the firm belief that a country like India, which has a rich heritage in alternative medicine, needs to foster the practice. Furthermore, poor people who cannot afford allopathic medicine can benefit from alternate practices. While doing the course, Satheesh was clear that he would go to tribal localities and serve the people there. He would help them maintain good health. This might look like a contradiction, because you would expect tribal people to be expert in the traditional cure systems that their tribes practiced over generations. The advantage of having a trained medical professional helps to expedite the cure process. Furthermore, traditional practices depend on hunches, whereas trained professionals are guided by the depth of their knowledge and the learning they derive from the cumulative experiences of others.

After passing out as an ayurvedic doctor from Coimbatore, Satheesh decided to join a social work project at Changlang district of Arunachal Pradesh. Most of the northeastern states in India require support, as they lie amidst mountain ranges and poor infrastructure places severe limitations on development. He joined a project called Arul Jyoti, which served the tribal rural people. Satheesh was there for two years and took no salary from the project owners. However, they took care of all of his requirements. He covered 10 tribal villages by helping them meet their healthcare requirements in a limited way.

Trigger: Though Satheesh had a childhood ambition of associating himself with the social sector, the experience in Arunachal Pradesh really helped him to assess his potential for serving tribal Indians. After two years of service there, he moved to Ooty, in the Nilgiri Hills of Tamil Nadu. The Nilgiri Hills are a mountain range with a long tribal tradition and a recent history, going back over two centuries, of exposure to the outer world. Satheesh was fully aware of the area's potential as he studied in Coimbatore, which is an adjourning district. He joined as a lecturer at the J. S. S College of Naturopathy and Yogic Sciences and served there for a few years. This is a unique institution, and the experience was very exciting for the young Satheesh.

During this period, he connected with Shyam Gupta, founder of the Ekal Vidyalaya Movement (www.ekal.org). He drew inspiration from the work of this movement. To digress here, readers may note here that a person needs not just a sense of social entrepreneurship, but also a lot of grit and comment to play the part of a social leader when building an organization in a particular location. It was indeed commendable of Shyam Gupta that he identified Satheesh for such a leadership position. It is interesting to see how Satheesh seized this opportunity with dedication and developed a carving to promote social welfare in tribal areas.

Satheesh mentions that it was his wife who was first hooked on Ekal Vidyalaya. Satheesh's wife is also a school worker. She hails from his hometown and knew him from childhood. Her family is also involved in social work and nation building through small and meaningful interventions. Satheesh's wife started spending two to three days a week on Ekal Vidyalaya Foundation work, and Satheesh took pains to find out and understand in detail the impact that he could make. After five years, Satheesh got more deeply involved as a fulltime associate in Ekal Foundation.

Opportunities: Ekal Vidyalaya focuses on delivering primary informal education programs to tribal and other underprivileged communities in rural India. Satheesh gave up his medical practice to educate tribal children. Since Ekal Vidyalaya goes beyond mere literacy, Satheesh was able to participate in its goal of achieving the national Minimum Level of Learning (MLL) standards for its students as well as enabling empowerment of the village community to seek and work on ways to achieve self-development. Ekal Vidyalaya solicits complete involvement of the local community, and this gave Satheesh a lot of opportunity to work on a broader spectrum.

Furthermore, the schools are also oriented to make children and villagers aware of basic health and hygiene concepts. Satheesh found this a wonderful opportunity to utilize his capabilities. Teachers at the Vidyalaya are local youth who have completed some formal education. The teachers are selected and trained by Ekal Vidyalaya. Satheesh involved himself in every nook and corner of every tribal village in the Nilgiri mountain range. The infrastructural facilities for the schools are minimal. In some cases, the classes are held in the shade of a tree, or a verandah of the local temple or community hall. Apart from becoming an educational hub, the Ekal teacher interacts with villagers and contributes to the participatory approach and development of the village. For a long time, Satheesh was instrumental in close work with the teachers. Often, schools had a single teacher. Thus, Ekal Vidyalayas are also having a transformational influence on rural and tribal communities, and Satheesh's role has been very important in building up the network in Tamil Nadu.

In Recognition of practical needs, Ekal has set up a well-designed hierarchical system. For every sub-cluster (10-school unit), cluster (30-school unit), sub-area (90-school unit) and area (270-school unit), there are committees to oversee the functioning of the schools and the activities associated with health care, development and empowerment education. The involvement of the locals at every level is based on their commitment and urge to help the people around them. The sense of community development has now permeated at the national and global levels. Over the years, Satheesh assumed increasing responsibility for the organization and groomed people at various levels to strengthen the reach to grassroots.

At present, Satheesh is mainly responsible for fund management and for coordination with investors on progress of the project. His current activities are focused on building investor confidence so that the initiatives are seamlessly integrated. He presently handles the North American market. He feels that there is an immense opportunity for a person like him to demonstrate professional acumen in serving tribal children and villagers.

Grooms talents: One of the passionate engagements of Satheesh is to groom talented social workers in his project area. He is now responsible at the organizational level for ensuring effectiveness of all programs and for managing funds, especially from North America.

Here, it is worth mentioning Madhavan, who was attracted by the Ekal concept and its implementation. Before long, Madhavan decided to support the project. Satheesh played a key role in mentoring Madhavan. Madhavan is a professional who works in the area of content development and management. He used to work for a leading publishing house and an IT company. His specialization is customizing the needs of first-time learners. The initiative of Ekal and Satheesh attracted Madhavan enough to cause him to commit his full time to develop content and learning tools for tribal children. Madhavan also realized that the reward from integrating value systems in learning is more important than earning pecuniary benefits. Though Satheesh and Madhavan are two among a number of social workers implementing education-oriented movements, their leadership plays an important role. Satheesh played a significant role in synchronizing Madhavan's desire with that of Ekal's.

This author feels obliged to mention an interesting couple who have dedicated their lives to the Ekal system. Satheesh identified and mentored them from their early days. Sathyamani is from a tribal village near Masinagudi (http://www.masinagudi.com/), where sightings of boars, elephants and panthers are common. Children of the area learn to merge into these natural habitats while at the same time they reach out and grow to be meaningful citizens. The alternative is to live and die as a tribal, with few opportunities to experience the world.

The organization of Ekal Vidyalaya influenced Sathyamani, who was a student there. The leadership of Satheesh particularly impressed her. She decided to take up a career of serving her fellow humans in and around her village, and she became quite popular because of her social work. Looking at her commitment, Satheesh encouraged her to visualize a larger role for herself and assume responsibilities accordingly. She is married to Anandan Kalidasan, who has a similar background. Both of them now manage the Ekal Chennai office. They travel the length and breadth of the country to train teachers and administrators in delivery of the Ekal programs. Satheesh is proud that the couple as a team travel for about 22-25 days in a month. Their office is in their small home in Chennai. They earn what most people would consider meager salaries. Their dream is to impact their fellow tribals, who have less or no access to development initiatives. According to them, by following the footsteps of Satheesh, they can have a meaningful impact on the lives of many people.

Other examples of people with talents who were groomed are Shankar in Kollimalai region, near Salem, and Saritha, from the same village as Sathyamani. These social workers are now busy travelling to a number of villages to administer Ekal projects under Satheesh's guidance. Satheesh avers that one can build such a dedicated team only through trust, love and affection. He feels it is necessary to treat team members as part of the family. Their leader should participate in their welfare. They require demonstrations of simplicity and need to see action that is faithful to the lessons that are preached.

Satheesh conducts a lot of leadership grooming exercises. He conducts motivational camps and takes his team on visits to successful people. One of the places he makes sure they become familiar with is Sri Sarada Ashram, Ulunderpet, Tamil Nadu (http://www.srisaradaashram. org) (Exhibit 1).

Exhibit 1 Sri Sarada Ashram

The initiative of Swami Anantananda, an ordinary person in his pre-monastic life, was responsible for launching Sri Sarada Ashram. He was a university first rank holder and wanted to do something beyond working for materialistic things in life. He reached the Sri Ramakrishna Mutt and took the spiritual path for salvation at Vellimalai.

He started a school with three students in a rented, dilapidated building. He highly impressed Yatiswari Ramakrishnapriya Amba, another person who had been captivated by spiritual thoughts. Along with three other sisters, she joined the school and converted it to a ladies' ashram. She took up multiple roles, including cook, caretaker, teacher and headmistress. She played almost all the roles from matron to manager. Under the leadership of Yatiswari Ramakrishnapriya Amba, the President of Sri Sarada Ashram, a team of 45 well-educated *sanyasin* sisters has been engaged in social work. The sisters of the *ashram* come from different backgrounds, and hail from different parts of Tamil Nadu. They are a highly qualified team consisting of eight engineers, one lady with a doctorate and many post-graduates in various fields of specialty.

The *ashram* was established with the core objectives of promoting and developing the poor and backward villages by providing quality education, affordable healthcare, cultural and socio-economic development activities, agricultural development and much needed, timely relief during natural disasters. Over 1,500 students and 1,000 women are given schooling, vocational training and job-oriented career coaching annually.

Source: http://www.srisaradaashram.org. Accessed on January 1, 2014.

Family support: It is inspiring to learn about the family guidance Satheesh received in his childhood. His father always encouraged him to attend social programmes. He learned a lot from his father on the habits of developmental leaders and dreamt of becoming one. Frugality and prudence are the major virtues of such leaders. They do not given importance to personal wealth creation for the self and the family. It was a pleasant surprise that Satheesh's spouse has similar traits. Satheesh's sister is also an important motivator, and is associated with his developmental activities.

The concept of working as an extended family was very important for Satheesh to be successful. A few instances would substantiate this statement. When Sathyamani's marriage to Kalidas Anandan was proposed, her parents, of typical tribal origin, opposed the proposal. Satheesh and his wife literally lived for a few days in Sathyamani's house, convinced her parents on the merit of this proposal and made them agree to it. This effort by Satheesh and his wife aimed at bringing about the happy union of a couple. Similarly, there was a time when Shankar of Kollimalai faced an obstacle to his continuing with social work, as his family felt that as though he was an adult, he was not supporting the family. Satheesh treated their family as his own and took up all responsibility for the education of Shankar's siblings, which made the family happy. The moral here is that social work cannot be undertaken at the cost of family, and one need not necessarily become a monk to serve society. Not everyone is capable of living life as a monk. One can be dedicated to the family as well as part of a team that builds up a solid social movement, as Satheesh and his family demonstrated.

Conclusion: It is not necessary to think and plan on a big scale to carry out social sector projects. There is abundant scope to align with an existing movement in the specific geographical area with which one is comfortable. After settling down, there is scope for scaling up operations and assuming larger responsibilities like any other promoter in any other cause, and drive the project forward towards a very large social coverage. In the process, one can groom many other social workers who could support and carry on the dream of serving society. Backward societies, like those of the tribal of India, would gain immeasurably if more spirited and committed professionals like Satheesh take to the social sector!

CHAPTER 10

Get inspired and rejuvenated:
G. V. Subramanian, Founder, Sadguru
Sri Gnanananda Seva Trust

GVS with his wife Anuradha

Introduction: Hard work and robust common sense are natural for someone who has travelled the long way from being a mediocre student to a successful banker. G.V. Subramanian (GVS) deployed precisely these two great assets of his to become a senior management professional in India's central bank, the Reserve Bank of India (RBI) and later with its wholly owned body the National Housing Bank. And these were the prime resources he adapted and used for his dream project—Swami Vivekananda Rural Community College or SVRCC—when he decided to become a social worker. Rarely does one come across people like GVS who listen to their conscience and speak and act with deep commitment and ownership for social causes.

GVS says it was divine direction that got him working for the benefit of the youth of this country. Swami Vivekananda and Roosevelt have spoken about the power of youth and the need to ignite the spark in them: and it is folks like GVS who do what these great men have envisioned about youth energy. How a simple person like GVS was inspired to serve society and the odds he faced in realizing his dream forms the rest of this absorbing story.

Early days: GVS was born in Mumbai and lived his early days at Kalyan, a distant suburb of Mumbai. An average student, he demonstrated right from his boyhood excellent commonsense and analytical skills, the power of introspection and the ability to communicate effectively even during the most stressful of times. His father ran a small business and could just about make ends meet. GVS had two elder sisters and they formed a close-knit family.

One of his elder sisters was suddenly bedridden; and she passed away. This drained the family emotionally. GVS's father was also concerned that GVS was not achieving a higher level of academic performance that was vital those days for security in life.

After school, GVS worked in a factory while pursuing his graduation in chemistry with success. He then passed a competitive examination and joined RBI. He worked hard and became an Assistant General Manager. He married Anuradha, also from Mumbai, and was blessed with three sons. After his early years at Mumbai, GVS had a long stint in Delhi and a shorter period in Bangalore.

Even at work he always thought out of the box and looked for opportunities to achieve an independent identity. Spiritual by nature, GVS read a lot of books on Vedanta. He believed in being honest, sincere and totally committed to whatever he was doing.

One day while in Delhi GVS happened to visit the famous temple of Malai Mandir. It was a Sunday evening and his attention was drawn to some soul-stirring singing by a small band of devotees. He inquired and learnt that they were singing Thiruppugazh, in praise of Lord Subrahmanya. The music so moved GVS that he decided to learn

Thiruppugazh. GVS struggled initially, having had no formal training in traditional Carnatic music. However, by virtue of his devotion and hard work he soon began singing with ease and in tune.

Thiruppugazh awakened in him the realization that human life is very precious and short and should not be frittered away. He understood the transitory nature of the material comforts and pleasures of life. The profound influence of Thiruppugazh gave GVS a new direction in life.

The trigger: In the mid-90s GVS reflected frequently on how the society around him had helped him succeed in life despite his shortcomings. He increasingly felt it was time he gave back to the society as some kind of thanks giving.

One eventful day GVS was travelling in a train to New Delhi with his wife. He met Reverend Fr. (Dr.) Xavier Alphonse, former Principal of Loyola College, Chennai. The Reverend is the Founder Director of the Indian Centre for Research and Development of Community Education (ICRDCE), Chennai. He talked about community colleges and about how he was working to developing community education in India.

GVS told him that he was excited by the concept and had been envisioning doing something along those lines in Pondicherry (now Puducherry). Fr. Alphonse did not take him seriously then, but for GVS it was a defining moment. He had always thought that the best way to serve the society was to reclaim poor youth who drop out of school and out of normal life, but his path ahead had been unclear until that meeting.

Soon after his interaction with the Reverend, he wanted to go ahead actively with the seed of the idea sown firmly in his mind. Most of his relatives and friends believed that he was being outrageous in pursuing such a dream when he had a plum job and was living a decent life with social and economic security. But for GVS the bell had truly tolled.

Times of apprehension and dismay: GVS owned an apartment at Mumbai in which he lived with his family. His two younger sons were still students. Nevertheless he took voluntary retirement in June 2003, eight years ahead of time and moved with his family to Chennai. He sold his flat at Mumbai and used his savings to buy some land in Pondicherry.

Though he was still short of the money needed for the land, his determination and connections got him the support he needed. He went through a tough time, when he had to give up possessions like his car and chauffeur. He used public transport to travel when meeting people to solicit support.

Many of his friends could not understand why he was doing this. But GVS believed that the hand of God would guide him constantly through timely intervention of benefactors—and that was what happened. The most notable of these benefactors was a well-placed company executive from Singapore who met him and listened to his plan.

The gentleman visited Pondicherry with his family and after getting familiar with GVS' vision, donated a substantial sum of money to enable completion of the land purchase. The saga continued in the same vein month after month. The persuasive skills of GVS and the good-hearted support of friends started transforming his dream into reality, albeit slowly.

GVS mentions that he motivated himself every day while at his prayers by visualizing the community college he wanted to build. He felt he was going to touch thousands of school dropouts and make their lives meaningful. Probably the power of this vision is what gave him energy!

The groundwork: GVS was a total stranger in the village he had chosen for his project. Hence he was not able to get the required local support. He went around and met all the key personalities like the village officers, local leaders, community heads and other individuals. Though many of them were not clear about his game plan, he got encouragement all around. He launched the college in a thatched shed and moved to a house in the locality.

He then started relentlessly to evangelize his concept. He spoke to auto rickshaw drivers and visited hair stylists' shops and various other places, including telephone booths to propagate his idea. He went to villages in a 30 km radius and discussed his project with people there.

But the local youth and their parents—the target group, so to say—were unappreciative.

GVS persevered and over the next few months managed to get the minimum number of students required to start the first batch in July 2008. He began with courses on refrigeration and AC mechanism, DTP and tailoring, and nursing assistance courses so that girls could benefit.

A parallel challenge was the need for qualified faculty members and the resources for teaching aids. He had only a stethoscope and a blood pressure monitor, for instance, for the nursing assistance program. A doctor friend from Chennai had given these equipment and paved the way to start the classes.

For the funding, GVS had an ingenious idea. He invited and got visitors to Pondicherry every weekend to study and understand his mission. These were his friends and contacts from Mumbai, Chennai, Delhi and elsewhere. He would take them to the community college site and share his thoughts and ask them to chip in. In the first three years this is how he built strength and visibility to the project, and financial muscle. Such was his infectious enthusiasm and captivating imagery that the guests could not help responding warmly and productively.

The alchemist: GVS is truly a gifted alchemist, creating a gem out of every student who comes into SVRCC. He gives us here, in his own words, some of his experiences which are at once a window to his own character as well.

There was one student named Sarada. She had been married very young and had two children. Her husband was a daily wage earner and an alcoholic. She had to do hard labor to survive and feed her children. She connected with the community college when she came to work there as a laborer. GVS admitted her to the college and mentored her. Sarada used to get up at 4 a.m. and read for about an hour and half. Then she would cook for the family and send her husband to work and her children to school. She would cycle to the college and back. This continued till she completed the nursing course. She is now a staff nurse at a medical college hospital.

Sheila was from a fishermen's community, and her parents were of the view that she should get married and have her own family. But Sheila wanted to be independent and support her parents even if she got married. GVS visited her village and talked to her parents and close relatives on a number of occasions and convinced the family to agree to her idea of becoming a nursing assistant. They even decided to drop her at the college and pick her up every day. Today, the girl works as a staff nurse and earns around rupees ten thousand per month.

Sharif is another gem of the community college. His father was an agricultural laborer and was barely able to survive. After failing in 10th grade Sharif had almost become an aimless vagabond. He joined the community college and studied hard to become an AC technician. Sharif now works in the Middle East and supports his family.

GVS has fashioned many such gems. The author met a male student who commuted for three and half hours each way to do a course at SVRCC. This boy is confidence personified now, and is clearly a spark that has been ignited. He wants to set up his own garage. Asked how he plans to do that, he says that he draws inspiration from his mentor, GVS!

About 500 students have passed out so far from this college. This may not compare with the number of students that regular educational institutions produce every year. However, what one has to consider is GVS's interest in getting school dropouts with no hope back into the mainstream as sensible, result-oriented and focused youngsters. The college now has a three-level state-of-the-art facility in Keezhputhupattu village near Puducherry that can train 1,000 students per year in up to 18 trades or professions. The building costing over Rs. 35 million has been constructed entirely with hard-earned donations and contributions from socially conscious philanthropists and corporate houses.

GVS has ensured continuity for his institution by forming a trust with 14 more community-conscious persons and getting all matters related to the college discussed and decided by the trust in formal and informal meetings. The documentation of all actions, decisions, finances and operations is meticulous, to say the least. This is governance at its best.

One should look at the towering impact GVS has on youth and their parents by giving them an option to revitalize their life. It is not just the tangible aspects of the project that are important; it is his burning desire to carefully nurture youth, like a dedicated gardener with his roses and shape them that is worth highlighting! It is not social entrepreneurship that distinguishes GVS from others. It is his touch of humility and humanity in encouraging the deprived to pursue a path of resurrection to a new life.

Virtues that carry: GVS believes certain virtues are required if one has to render social service in the field of vocational education. He lists these as: connecting, evangelizing, action, consensus and demonstration. If even one of these virtues is missing, success in community development will elude you.

Connecting: One needs to connect with people who can share time, touch, treasure or talent, or any combination of these ingredients. It is important to get people who are down to earth and have been successful. When his students see these successes, they are inspired.

Evangelizing: You cannot and should not stop talking about the theme and the goal that you are pursuing, at the right forums and to the right people.

Action: Action speaks louder than words and evangelizing without action consistent with the idea is useless. More importantly, GVS says it is action that connects him with God.

Consensus: GVS is known to give equal respect to all stakeholders. His students, their parents, visitors and donors all receive the same degree of attention. He brings this virtue of consensus also in the way he runs the trust matters—with transparency, orderly documentation, discipline and total honesty.

Demonstration: GVS involves his students in community work, and works along with them. He believes that more than saying, doing and showing impacts youth deeper.

You get an object lesson in how to successfully pilot an NGO when you see GVS as an embodiment of these five vital virtues, and it is little wonder he has done so much in so short a time.

Family support: The humble person he is, GVS attributes a lot of the credit to his family and their staunch support. And he is right: his wife Anuradha (Anu) is a pillar of strength in his endeavors. From the day she married him she synchronized her life with his. They respect each other's independence and still work together comfortably. When GVS wanted to sell his flat, resign his job and put all his savings into his dream, Anu never hesitated. She unquestioningly fell in with the dream and in her practical no-nonsense way started thinking out the next steps.

Anu thanks her father for grooming her in the art of giving. She brings a lot of positive energy to GVS, her three sons and the students of SVRCC.

GVS's mother has been another great support. When GVS resigned his job ahead of time she was old and had some health challenges but never complained about the inconveniences of not having a car or comfort support system. On the other hand, she encouraged GVS to pursue his mission and managed the house and her grandchildren with Anu's support while GVS was out and about.

An understanding and supportive family is a key factor in the successful pursuit of missions of mercy like SVRCC.

A final word about the man and his mission: India is a country where there is a lot of youth power and all demographic indexes support the concept of using this youth power for growth. However, the existing infrastructure and system are inadequate for effectively harnessing the potential of youth. Welcome to the world of community education, of which GVS and Swami Vivekananda Rural Community College are a part.

GVS's institution today attracts members of the national and international social work community to study his success and its replication potential. For a man to have relinquished his comfort zone to pursue his dream is a phenomenal achievement. But GVS is not one to rest on his laurels. He is working 24X7 to expand his operations to achieve a much larger area of impact.

Our society can become a far better place to live only with the help of the youth that people like GVS harness, rejuvenate and inspire. And the very same youth can destroy a civilization if left uncared for. We need many GVSs in our midst because the country's youth population is truly prodigious and India's economic goal is to become a superpower. May more GVSs flower, may his tribe increase!

CHAPTER 11

Educating children in villages: Shadab Hassan, Founder, Director, H.H.High School, Brambe

Introduction: It is challenging enough to be born to a humble family in a rural village, especially in a developing country like India. When a person without ambition is born in such a place, he would find it difficult to avoid going through life whiling away time, even as his urban counterparts go to school. If such a person has a bit more discipline, he may become a child laborer. On the other hand, there are those people who fight all odds to achieve an education in a town. They may need some good fortune in getting someone to give them a ride every day to school and back. If they are extraordinarily fortunate, they may find some relatives or friends who are kind enough to provide them accommodation and food, thus enabling them to avoid their daily commute. Normally, such people are keen to move up in life and benefit themselves, their immediate families and their proximate societies. There are innumerable cases of such people struggling through to become doctors, civil servants or IT professionals and settle down for good.

Here is one such person, Shahid Shadab Hassan, who came from a humble background, climbed his way to a leading institute for his Master's in Business Administration and decided to dedicate his career to building up school education in his home village, 20 km away from Ranchi, the capital of Jharkhand.

Childhood days: Though Shadab was born in Ranchi, he spent his initial childhood days in Brambe until he started going to school. His family is one of those typical traditional families of rural India. His grandfather, (Late) Hamid Hassan, was a freedom fighter. His father, Dr. Shahid Hassan during his school days did odd jobs like selling balloons and setting up bicycle stand in the village. The village had no school, but he was determined to study and come up in life. He somehow managed to complete his school and used to go on free rides with his uncle, who was a mechanic working in a garage for a businessman in Ranchi. He grew up to become a professor, and is now imparting knowledge in the Post Graduate Department of Psychology at Ranchi University.

His father's efforts enabled Shadab to enjoy better comfort in life. Though the family lived in Brambe in the initial years of his childhood, they later moved to Ranchi. This helped Shadab to obtain superior education at one of the best schools and colleges at Ranchi. However, he usually spent weekends at Brambe with his family. He felt disturbed by how his cousins and friends lacked the schooling opportunities he was availing. His grandfather and father were his heroes. In fact, his grandfather was a father figure for the whole village for having had the courage to educate his son. He was unassuming, but in high demand in his society because of his leadership and ability to mentor families and help them resolve their issues. Almost as a hereditary trait, this built up aspirations in Shadab to do good for the society that looked up to his family and to respond in all possible ways to meet the needs of the people of Brambe.

Shadab was a boy scout at the school and liked going on service-oriented trips to schools where specially abled children were studying. These trips taught him compassion, and he began to think in terms of helping the specially abled children to study better.

Trigger to make a difference: It pained Shadab to see children doing odd jobs in his village. It is not only illegal to make children work in stalls and households, it also cheapens the value of human resources in the economy through inappropriate deployment of resources for less productive work. If this trend is to be broken, the "Right to Education" policy must be implemented with more vigor, and village populations must be made to absorb and accept the concept of sending children to school. Shadab felt that there was a lot of propaganda about compulsory education, but there was no matching effort at ground levels. Second, he also felt that a drive to improve literacy could not be handled by the government alone. The effort needs social entrepreneurs and individuals with a social bent of mind and a determination to build future of India to jump onto the bandwagon. Shadab was influenced by Gandhian thought. He said, "India's freedom struggle triggered commitment not only from Indians in urban areas but also from the people of rural India. Only when everyone gets involved on such a scale transformational change of society will happen. Otherwise, the deprived would continue to stay in their rut. Intervention through education is important to harness youth power and take advantage of the demographic quotient. "I felt that I must do something at my level which could impact my village and a few more villages around. More importantly, I would be happy if I could motivate more youths to commit themselves for a social cause." These are excellent words of wisdom from Shadab who is in his mid-twenties, a young age.

Initial steps for a concrete action: About to complete his Master's, Shadab found himself in a catch-22 situation. He could opt to work at some job for five years or more and save enough money to start a school at his village. However, his inner voice told him that if he delayed the school plan by five years, many of the children in his village and other villages around would be deprived of a potentially life-changing opportunity. Moreover, whatever money he managed to save in five years would at best be seed capital; he would have to raise much more money to finance a complete school. In any case, a financial management skill set would be required of him in the longer term. He decided to ignore the jobs available through placement at the college campus and launched his project to set up a school in Brambe.

He first started the school in a small plot of land owned by his family. There was no proper building or infrastructure. His mother gave him a lot of confidence and support. There was no classroom, board or teacher. The school lacked other support services. He enrolled a few students and enlisted the services of a few like-minded friends who wanted to teach in their leisure times. He selected a few of them and initially engaged them in fulltime teaching. He started off on January 16, 2010, with open-air classrooms, no desks, no chairs, no benches. Instead he had a couple of woven carpets hired on rent, a few black boards, a semi-constructed structure and the willingness to teach. From that humble beginning with 80 kids, he was able to steadily build up this idea of social improvement. As of September 2013, the school had around 500 students enrolled for the ongoing academic year.

Shadab says, "In a social venture, it is not starting an initiative but keeping it going that is the challenge. Once started, it must be sustained, as expectations from the beneficiaries are high. Hence, it is important to keep this in mind and work at running an institution, not a job or an alternate career. Second, unlike private businesses, which face the challenges of tough competition, in social ventures there is no competition. The challenge for me is to ensure that my coworkers stay equally excited day in and day out so that all of us, as a team, bring the same kind of energy and spirits and take the initiative ahead. That was my prime focus in the initial days".

Challenges faced: Shadab faced many challenges in keeping the school going. Every idea faced challenges to its implementation. First, there was no culture or tradition of sending children to school in his village.

People were poor, and their priority was not schools. He had to go on a door-to-door campaign pleading with parents to send their children to school. One of the obvious questions he had to answer was, what would the children do after schooling? Though a better answer would come with experience, Shadab had to speak in general terms, giving pep talks on the benefits of education. He also used this campaign to understand the expectations of the people around him. Initially, about 30 students were willing to register with the school. It was not easy, as there were rumors about his intentions behind wanting the children to study. He was literally seen as a spoiler of the labor quotient. The only thing that sustained him in approaching the families and fighting their fear of the "unknown" was his family background and the goodwill his grandfather carried. In fact, Shadab named the school after his grandfather. The first challenge to be faced was admissions.

The single parent or extremely poor kids were taught absolutely free of cost, but the second challenge was collecting a fee of Rs. 100 per student per month from those who could pay. Though this was a nominal fee, it was something folks could ill afford in this kind of village in India. But then, how could Shadab run the school without revenue? Moreover, he also felt that collecting a fee was important because that brought the onus onto the family to support their children's education and stay inquisitive about what the children were getting in return for the money spent. Typically, many of these families would not know whether their children were really going to school, and even when the children were going to school, they may not bother to actually make the effort and learn. Shadab had to insist on payment of fees. But as Shadab puts it to the parents, he always said, "If a child does well, HE is responsible. If he doesn't, WE are responsible." This assurance imposed a very high demand on him and his teachers. He first had to win the support of his teachers. However, he incentivized fee payment by using certain novel means. If parents did not have the money to pay immediately, they could pay whenever they did get money. He also gave free education to the third child in a family, especially if girl students accompanied a boy student. He also felt the need to support children who were orphans or have single parents, especially mothers. He made education free for them. It may be noted here that at least 20% of the children in the school studied absolutely free of cost.

He also made some innovative moves to educate the illiterate rural women on the importance of education. He started a program called "Maatri" for this purpose. Volunteers reached households and taught women to read and write. The women of Brambe and the surrounding villages were deeply appreciative of this effort. Shadab showed visionary thinking in getting even elders to read and write without looking for government support. They in turn supported Shadab in his mission—his social venture of running a school.

The third challenge was finding teachers and volunteers. There were quite a few volunteers who were willing to come from Ranchi to Brambe to teach. The major issue was that they could come only at odd timings, whenever they were free, whereas schools have to operate on fixed schedules. While Shadab initially recruited a few teachers, he and his mother also had to teach full time at the school. This consumed a lot of his time and adversely affected his efforts to raise funds and develop the school further. He was of the view that if he set up the model with the right momentum, building up further could happen later.

The fourth challenge was getting students and parents to spend on books. He recommended the parents to buy textbooks at the full prices and resell them at the end of the year at half value. Thus, they would benefit by half the cost of the books, while the subsequent buyers would also benefit just as much. Though these issues may look very simple, he had to work personally on even such mundane activities to make the movement successful.

Far more enterprising at a village: Shadab set up means of having online classrooms. There was no sophistication involved. He kept a LCD monitor on a table and connected it to his laptop. He also arranged external speakers and cameras. He requested those volunteers who could not come to the school to logon and teach over video calls. At times, such sessions lasted three hours. This was a phenomenal approach in a rural school—scheduling with limited resources using technology was an amazing approach that demonstrated his commitment and innovation in driving learning through reach-out programs. It could enable broad bases for children's learning and also motivate them. He ensured that any sponsor who spends on a child's education could come online and observe the progress of the program. All these steps demonstrate Shadab's ability to convert instincts into action for a larger purpose.

Shadab participated in the Jagriti Yatra—2012. The Jagriti Yatra is an annual train journey taken by highly motivated young Indians. It is organized by the Jagriti Sewa Sansthan, a non-governmental organization that promotes entrepreneurship. This specially hired 18-wagon train takes 450 young men and women, including students, and entrepreneurs, including a few rural entrepreneurs. Selection is based on a highly competitive selection process. During the Yatra, Shadab was given an opportunity to address all the other passengers and tell them about himself and his initiative. As he moved through the compartments of the train as it was on the move, he met with a professional from Google's India office based in Bangalore. This person got excited by Shadab's initiatives, and after the Yatra, a team of Google employees from Bangalore volunteered to teach the school kids at Brambe over Google Hangout. The fact that he achieved all of this within three years of starting the school shows Shadab's spirit and drive.

Shadab made sure that the children had fun while learning. He screened several educational, motivational or animated movies for the school children. He also ensured more all-round learning by encouraging the students to participate in Interschool competitions. It may be worth noting here that the school students won the 2nd prizes in the Inter School Quiz competition organized by the Jharkhand government in February, 2010, merely a month after it was started. He took the students out to Ranchi to expose them to real-world concepts and events, including visit to film festivals, science city, State museum etc. He demonstrated excellent leadership traits in building up the futures of these children. The big moment came when former President of India, Dr. A.P.J. Abdul Kalam, recognized his efforts and felicitated him with

Yuva Prabhodhan during the launch of 'What Can I Give Mission' in Jharkhand.

Shadab constantly monitors and encourages his students to outperform themselves each day. He draws the attention of the media to the children when they do exceptionally well. In particular, the performances of girl students have attracted great attention, as they scored high marks. Shadab feels the school will revolutionize the village, bringing about the right thinking and approaches towards ensuring decent livelihood prospects for children, instead of encouraging child labor.

Apart from purely academic aspects, he also focuses on making sure that the children develop good health and hygiene practices. He conducts free health checkup camps and invites qualified people to come and speak of good preventive care and appropriate habits for good health. Furthermore, one of the important initiatives he has undertaken is 'Freedom Heroes'. This initiative recognizes and felicitates ordinary people who have shown extraordinary traits and have helped bring a positive change in and around the school. He believes that rather than worshiping film heroes, it is more important for the children to identify real life heroes and be enthused by them and follow their footsteps. At times, he prefers less-known performers because they strike a chord easily with the students. Such thinking is really worth emulating.

Family support: His family has been of great support. His parents and his wife stood by him, allowing him to pursue his ambition to build a school as a social venture actively. Additionally, his mother got directly involved in the school's operations right from the beginning. His wife Neha, who is an Assistant Professor in the Central University of Jharkhand supported him in every possible way and this made for great moral support for Shadab, and proved the family's commitment to progressive action and uplifting of the society to the villagers.

Conclusion: Shadab strongly believes in action, because he senses that deeds are worth more than words. He also believes that selective insulation from the rest of the world is important for success, and that sometimes one needs to be selfish to pursue what one desires. He narrated an event when a well-placed person in society denounced him and his actions, mentioning publicly that his efforts to provide education to children were of no use. Shadab never gets swayed by such comments and stays clearly entrenched in his initiatives and actions. He advises other youth to undertake similar socially beneficial work wherever they are and in whatever way they think they can impact society most. This world would improve in leaps and bounds if only more Shadabs surface.

CHAPTER 12

Giving what could not be had: C.Saravanan, Founder, Manam Malarattum

Introduction: In the early stages of development of a society, food availability, clothing and shelter were the minimal criteria for humans to live with dignity. As society advances, it is expected that every social group should have access to education, opportunities to work, earn a living and access to a good health care system. However, if we were to look at the human development indicators for education, we would note that there are a few glaring anomalies in India. One, there is a significant difference among rural and urban achievements in the education sector in terms of parameters like school enrolment at the secondary and high levels. Second, there are differences in gender-wise registrations and dropouts, with boys ahead of girls. Third, there are wide variations for geographic locations. While some states are moving ahead appreciably, a few are still backward. Similarly, there are differences within a state. Even in Tamil Nadu, it can be seen that some districts are doing better on education-related parameters while others are lagging behind.

Undesirable impact: There could be umpteen reasons explaining why such discrepancies exist in the system. A number of initiatives by the government and by non-government social organizations are aimed at improving the level of education. It may be noted that discrepancies are more in the rural areas and wherever there is scope is mainly for government schools. Economics do not support private schools. Inadequate levels of literacy cause a number of undesirable impacts on society. First, because of lack of opportunities to achieve sufficient education, a large number of people are not suitable for the better jobs, and are forced to take to the more physical type of work that comes with low-earning potential. This feeds the vicious cycle of poverty and economic alienation leading to lack of educational opportunities, leading again to further poverty. This situation leads to social disruption, when youth become disgruntled and indulge in undesirable activities such as robbery and alcoholism. There are many places in tribal areas of the hills where the chances of indulgence in self-destructive activities such as resorting to alcohol and drugs are high. As a consequence, social evolution is slow, and marriages are not successful.

Saravanan, like many of us, was pained by the lack of opportunities faced by the poor and the way this phenomenon affected society adversely. A young Saravanan, in his early twenties, gathered the courage to work to give children impetus in their education through committed plans and efforts. This write up unfolds the story of Saravanan's drive to be meaningfully different.

Initial trigger: Saravanan grew up in a village in the orbit of a small town, Tiruppatur, near Katpadi in Vellore district. He came from a poor family and had his education at a government school. He always thought he needed more academic support and felt deprived as he was growing up. His family circumstances made him decide that it was critical to find employment. This led him to complete his diploma in electronics and communication engineering in Namakkal, a neighbouring town. He then worked as an apprentice in Hindustan Teleprinters Ltd for a year. Later, he worked at the Tamil Nadu Electricity Board for a year as trainee. He felt that he had not achieved enough by way of education and that he had not received enough opportunities.

He was an avid reader of religious books He was influenced by the writing of Swami Dayananda Saraswathi, especially *"Manam Malaratum"* (Let Hearts Blossom). He quit his job at the electricity board and began distributing books in nearby towns and villages. Saravanan realized that the best gift he could offer to society was to educate those people who needed it the most. He himself had been deprived of the right levels of education. He realized he could fill the void in him by offering opportunities to others and enabling them to realize their potential through his efforts. This kind of benevolent view in the tender twenties clearly reflects benevolent personality.

Saravanan thus answered his inner conscience's call to serve poor rural and tribal students who want to achieve more educationally, but did not have adequate support at home. One must try to understand this problem without casting aspirations on the stakeholders involved. First, government schools in remote villages find it difficult to get suitably qualified staff. Second, teachers find it difficult to commute to rural areas and, therefore, are less motivated. Third, classes are limited in size, inhibiting full realization of group potential. Finally, there is no additional support from outside the system to provide additional coaching and facilities for motivating both teachers and students.

Saravanan focused initially on addressing these issues with a concerted effort to mobilize resources locally and deploy them for the benefit of the students.

Perseverance yields! Saravanan first selected a few rural schools near Tiruppatur. When he approached the school authorities, they were disinterested on the grounds that they had already provided the best facilities and that their students could be overloaded. Furthermore, they also questioned Saravanan's intentions. They were not willing to give him access to infrastructure like classrooms.

Saravanan started networking closely in his chosen villages and in each, identified a common sheltered structure with lighting, where students could assemble. This could be an annex outside a residential house or a common purpose structure used by villagers to resolve their issues. He showed his commitment by teaching students. On observing his sustained efforts, villagers encouraged him. Students, too, started realizing the benefits. They could do their homework better with his support and also read as long as they wanted in a comfortable setting.

Soon, Saravanan was faced with two other growth-related issues. The first arose from his rising fame: on hearing of his initiative, students from several other villages wanted the same support. Some students came from villages as far away as 20 km to attend his classes. These villages were not well connected by bus services, and many of the students could not afford anything other than public transport. Saravanan had to consider the establishment of more study centres. This led to the other challenge.

The necessity of increasing the number of study centres was demand driven. Students and their parents convinced their local school authorities and other persons of influence to welcome him. They also supported him by providing a common space to run the classes. Saravanan's problem was identifying qualified instructors who could teach subjects for classes all the way up to the 12th grade. He developed a model to resolve this issue: he would identify a local resource who was at least a graduate and organize the training around him. Later in this article, we will discuss this model, its problems and the necessary resolutions. Saravanan's dream of enabling students to perform better was becoming reality.

However, hurdles are not just on the physical side! There were many emotional hindrances to overcome. His family did not approve of his idea. They thought that he had gone weird after reading religious writings and that his guilt over not having measured up in studies was prompting him to pursue social action. They were of the view that his model was not sustainable, and more importantly, that it would not enable to stay gainfully employed and earn a decent living.

Saravanan frequently quoted from religious texts and wanted to lead a life of purpose, rather than a life given to creating wealth. He was of the view that wealth did not necessarily consist of only tangible assets but also included the intangible values created by serving the needy. His mother was harsh with him. Quite a few of his critics made statements like, "A youth taking to social work individually is like someone trying to beautify the dead".

Saravanan did not allow his critics to dampen his spirits. On the positive side, there was one soul in his family he could bank on for total support. This was his grandmother, who encouraged him to listen to his conscience and do whatever made him happy. He went ahead with his chosen work relentlessly, giving it all of his personal time.

Passion for social entrepreneurship: Saravanan took the support of friends to expand his reach. They soon realized that their team was not sufficient, since continued growth demanded new skills to organize instructors, infrastructure, finance, establishing relationships and networking. Saravanan became aware that if his passion was to blossom into a larger initiative, he needed to become a social entrepreneur. The objective was not making a surplus cash flow for the sake of profit, but for reaching a large number of beneficiaries.

Saravanan registered a trust named *"Manam Malaratum"*. He received guidance from a swamiji and a few successful NGO promoters. He put his entire money and so did two of his friends! They connected with two NRIs from his district and were glad to support the initiative, trusting Saravanan's leadership skills.

Saravanan created his model to ensure students contributed nothing except their presence and studiousness. It is natural for funding stakeholders to say that if the beneficiaries are not paying some extent of fees, then the project may not be worth the effort. However, the problem here was, if asked to pay, the beneficiaries would stop attending the classes. Hence, the model clearly depended entirely on donors to support the initiative.

To give an idea of the magnitude we are talking about, Saravanan is presently extending his support to nearly 1,500 students in remote villages, 500 students in tribal areas and about 250 students studying in the highest grades, eleventh and twelfth. These efforts are spread over more than 80 locations. An instructor for the lower grades is paid about Rs. 3,500 per month and for the higher grades up to Rs. 5,000 per month. Thus, a lot of money is required, between rupees 30 and 40 lakhs per annum. Saravanan has been successfully managing this requirement for the last 12 years.

Sticking to core values:

There are certain ethical principles, like no payment of bribes and respect for all stakeholders' roles, which are fundamental to running his initiative. Saravanan never attempted to get an out of way official sanctions or permissions to run his mission. He did not permit the school's teachers or administrators to charge any kind of fees from students, as the services provided to students were completely free. For any additional efforts teachers contributed to his trust activities, he paid them separately from donated funds. He felt it necessary to demonstrate to his students that ethical values are of the utmost importance to succeed in life.

He is operating a CBSE school with classes up to the eighth grade near Tiruppatur. He claims that there have been no instances of collection of donations or fees other than those prescribed from the parents of students studying there. He is getting adequate support from the administration to run the school in a fair and just manner. He takes pride in mentioning that his trust has never paid a bribe for any of its activities.

Another principle he holds dear to heart is to respect the role of all stakeholders; all social activities must be undertaken through consensus and not in an atmosphere of conflict. Whenever he needs to convince the school administration, local leaders, parents or children on the merits of some issue, Saravanan first identifies their individual roles and responsibilities and then explains how his initiative would facilitate their mutual progress.

It may be most interesting to note his good work in the Jamunamuthur forest area in Thiruvannamalai district, which is a tribal area. Local children do not have adequate schooling facilities. Adults leave to seek work in other regions, leaving the children either in boarding schools or under the care of elders. There is some scope for them to get involved in undesirable acts. Though it is generally a well-disciplined community, it is important to give proper education and guidance to children to enable them to progress the right way in life. With the help of officials and elders, Saravanan initiated services to this community. He focused on inculcating high values in the youth, so that it would ensure proper growth in their lives. Today, he has more than 500 tribal students benefiting from the outreach activities. His core values of not conflicting with the community, but providing beneficiaries with higher levels of knowledge and growth opportunities are amazing. Though it is easy to appreciate an effort after it has come to fruition, it is less easy to see and appreciate the phenomenal level of initial struggle needed to make stakeholders understand the need and pursue necessary fieldwork without structured and institutional funding.

Frugality is another principle Saravanan follows and exemplifies. He conducts all of his activities with no frills and no extravagance. He believes that students must imbibe simplicity and humbleness while young and live their later lives by those standards. He is of the view that one must contribute to society without expecting any returns. He mentions the fact that no beneficiary is advised to repay and support the trust later, when well positioned in life. He believes that commitment to social causes must arise as the result of self-realization and must be voluntary. He is of the firm view that what one gives with good intentions multiplies and returns, though not necessarily from the original beneficiary.

Ability to see the big picture: Saravanan's greatest strength is his ability to see the big picture. There are now more than 1,000 engineers who were able to qualify because of the motivation and support given by him and his trust. He takes pleasure in mentioning that some of them qualified from the prestigious Anna University. A few of them have gone on to study medicine and become doctors. When asked about how they are giving back to their villages, Saravanan clarified that he does not focus his activities on reaping what he sows, but on improving the lot of deprived communities by facilitating better education. Of course, there are instances where a few of his beneficiaries who progressed to jobs in prestigious IT companies support him with their contributions.

In a sense, Saravanan is able to see the big picture of improving the economic lot of people in rural and tribal areas of India by enabling their wards to settle and prosper in developed regions of the country.

Conclusion: One need not be rich, educated and well connected to enable better education in rural and neglected areas. What one needs are a strong will and a kind heart to make life meaningful for others through humble acts. One will almost surely face organizational challenges such as identifying infrastructure and winning the approval of local authorities, school administrators and parents. However, if one moves with the conviction that his efforts will help to improve society, no problem is insurmountable! Saravanan has shown the way, even at the cost of his personal life: at 33 years of age, he is still unmarried.

Well, the more Saravanans there are, the more our youth, especially in the rural and neglected areas, are enabled to realize their dreams, and the more we can advance towards the goal of achieving high growth and equitable distribution of wealth across India.

CHAPTER 13

Making a difference for the downtrodden: V.murali, Managing Trustee, Kalaalayam

Introduction: Often, one comes across multifaceted personalities who would like to handle several different activities to impact the ecosystem around them. With such people, one would commonly come across clearly divergent interests, like sports and games or a couple of sports and games together with academic pursuits and later, a professional career. In the same way, one comes across artists who have unique capabilities in more than one area of specialization. Here we are discussing murali, a multifaceted personality, who is balancing the requirements of a job along with his interests in the social sector. Over the last two decades, he has committed himself to helping children who are downtrodden and deprived in some form or the other, mostly economic. Further, he is interested in the preservation of 64 traditional arts of India, which are right now specifically centred on selected locations.

Early days: murali was born as the youngest in a family of eight children. He has five sisters and two brothers. A native of Kumbakonam, he was born and brought up in Neyveli, a cosmopolitan township where his father was working. He had constraints in pursuing his higher education because of inadequate economic support. However, he managed to complete his graduation and took a job later in a public sector enterprise, the Chennai Petroleum Corporation Limited, at Chennai.

murali was born to a family where learning Sanskrit and Vedas was a routine task among various daily chores. He excelled in learning, and started taking an interest not only in learning but also in propagating his learning among others, even in his youth days. He often wondered whether learning Vedas and religious rituals was leading towards spirituality or towards parochial thinking. He asked his grandfather this question, who clarified that a true sense of religion lies in being open and benevolent and in encompassing one and all to achieve human oneness. At the same time, it is important to preserve traditions, as good spirits and learning must be passed down through the generations and most of such learning is through *gurukulams*.

Thus, murali's early life helped him to build his values and beliefs through a disciplined and religious family setting. The later helped him to serve society by creating harmony, preserving arts and traditions and providing equal opportunity of learning for the oppressed.

Trigger: About twenty years back, that is, in 1994, while commuting to work in a company bus, murali was passing through a locality called Madhavaram in Chennai. This is a thickly populated area which mostly comprises of people in the low-income group and those who are below the poverty line. murali was disturbed to see 18 children sitting on the road and studying in a free school. He observed this for three days and finally got down from his bus on the third day to probe further and explore if he could make some difference to those kids. He had laudable ambition and bold thinking. However, he was not sure how he could make it, as he was working in a public sector concern with a reasonable salary, and had a family with two daughters to support!

After consulting with his colleagues at CPCL, he decided that starting an evening school was the best way to go forward. In 1994, murali and a few of his friends started Kalaalayam in Chennai as a non-profit NGO working for a social cause. murali asserts that "Kalaalayam as an institution is secular, devoted to providing value-based purposeful education to the poor. It is a growing organization born of a burning desire to touch and mould the lives of deprived children and take them onto the path of success and accomplishment". The evening school at Madhavaram was the first of the network.

murali roped in more than 200 of his colleagues to contribute and support the activities. Currently, murali, through Kalaalayam, runs over 20 evening schools. The offerings include:

> ➤ Covering all school grades between LKG and +2, Kalaalayam's adopted students' fees are paid and they are provided with free notebooks, uniforms and other educational accessories. Thus far, around 20,500 students have benefited from Kalaalayam in more than 20 villages in getting educational aid and accessories.
> ➤ Evening schools are being established in each adopted village, wherein students are put through their syllabus by a Kalaalayam faculty member in the evening. In every village, a local faculty member is appointed to teach students.
> ➤ Needy students are helped with notebooks, computers or with any other schooling needs by linking the students with donors (http://www.kalaalayamtrust.org).

murali mentions that "As on June 2013, we had totally helped more than 20,500 students of various downtrodden villages/schools". This is an impressive effort for a public sector employee who had to balance work and desire to serve the downtrodden with the support of other trustees at CPCL, such as K. Pitchumani, V. Vasant Kumar and P. Rangaraj, as well as Prema Jeevanandham at BSNL, Trichy, not to mention so many other friends and colleagues. What has been important is the ability to provide subtle leadership and convert a vision into action!

There were certain focuses that murali was able to bring in from the beginning. The trustees decided that their assistance would go only to those who were poor and could not afford private schooling. All the children supported by them are either from corporation—or municipal-run schools. Second, a teacher must preferably be from the same locality, must be fairly educated and should support learning with some incentives and tools provided by them. Third, most of the centres are also supported by good health and soft issues through practice of yoga. murali has tied up with Krishnamachari Yoga Mandiram (KYM), leading yoga practice centre in Chennai, for employing trainers through whom children are taught yoga. Fourth, all children are imbued with good character and value systems by making prayer compulsory. The prayer is not oriented towards any religion or god. Each student is encouraged to choose his/her own faith centre, mediate and practice, focusing on that centre. Children are issued notebooks to write "Bhagawan Namas" which endows them with better discipline. This part of it is kept voluntary as murali believes in being secular and in demonstrating secularity in the field. This, according to murali, not only helps students achieve good values, but also boosts their ability to focus on a specific matter.

murali is nurturing grand plans for Kalaalayam by wishing to adopt a minimum of five tuition centres and a maximum of 25 centres in each of the 32 districts of Tamil Nadu and provide them with the required basic infrastructure. Students would be supported in education, basic computer knowledge and yoga. This grand plan would help him to reach more than 160,000 children across the state. He has been working on getting financial support, as he needs to go beyond the support of his colleagues at CPCL. He is looking at tie-ups with top corporates in each of the districts for setting up these centres. His thinking and zeal to achieve this is as commendable as his drive to help the children of the downtrodden sections of society. The challenge for him would be to identify next-level leaders and implementers among the trustees capable of taking his project forward. At the moment, murali has nurtured his initial trigger into a meaningful, sizeable initiative that he is able to run with the support of his colleagues. As he scales up, the challenge would be to create a truly social venture as well as the need for giving fulltime attention to that venture. A second challenge would be to establish an enduring set up that could surmount all problems associated with the pressure of handling delivery consistently at all the centres.

Blending social justice and religious activities: murali has studied the Vedas in a *gurukulam* at Kulithalai and he practices elaborate rituals even today. He is of the strong view that the secular fabric of the country can be maintained only through tolerance and by encouraging the individualism of each community. If he has to promote this belief as a social worker, he needs to practice what he preaches. Hence, he has prioritized observance of tolerance and individualism in all activities pursued by him. He also strongly feels that many communities are allowing their traditions to erode in their efforts to catch up with pecuniary demands and pressures. Even then, not all of them could achieve success. A large residual part of the community is under stress, as the demand for their services is dwindling and there are not many mentors and experts. To overcome this, there is a need for revival of such traditional practices and for encouraging them, especially in rural areas. For example, there is a proportionate decrease in availability of Vedic scholars in certain regions.

murali has initiated a trust by the name "Dharma Sanjeevinee Bhavanam" (Dharmic Revival Trust) (**http://www.dsbhavanam.in**), which focuses on support to and conservation of the 64 ancient arts of India. This is a larger goal, and the current set of activities include support to *veda patasalas, gow samarakshanam, bhagwan nama* bank, monumental temple renovation, astrology classes, divine renderings, free distribution of religious items and agro reforms. Action at the ground level requires a lot of coordination and support from different governmental agencies and local groups. For example, monumental temple renovation work is largely handled by government departments. If murali has to play a role in this activity, he has to work along with them and create space for his own contribution. Furthermore, questions could arise as to why such private initiative is required if a government set up is already in operation? The fact is that given his ability to garner local understanding of traditions and interests, murali is able to represent the government better and take government initiatives further. With God's grace, murali is setting a world record by installing a *nandhavanam* at Sri Vittal Rukmini Samsthan, Govindapuram, Kumbakonam, which is a remarkable sanctity for *nakshthra vrukshas* (star trees—each star representing 4 *padams*, totaling 108, with some more divine herbal saplings, adding up to around 130 trees, inclusive of *rudraksha* trees), under the agro reforms project.

Family and support: As mentioned earlier, murali belongs to a traditional family. He has struggled on his way up to economic freedom. His parents and siblings have always tried to instill good values in him and encouraged him, and gave him the confidence to help the needy even when he was young. His grandfather was a great scholar and his father has impacted him with Hari Hara *bhakthi*, while his mother blessed him in all he did, from an early age. His wife and two daughters are also supportive and encourage him to continue with his endeavors, irrespective of the limited time they get for themselves from him.

His friends are involved in his initiatives. A number of his colleagues at CPCL contribute to his educational activities. There are also experts with him as trustees in his interest to promote traditions across locations in Tamil Nadu. For example, well-known astrologer K. Pitchucmani is involved as a life trustee and encourages some of the children interested in astrology to learn it as a passion and spread the practice. murali believes that all children must pick up an alternate interest so that they have multiple options later in life, and must spread peace and harmony in society.

Conclusion: It is interesting to study and understand murali's trigger to help the poor with education, with *gow samrakshanam* and with the preservation of the herbal divine star trees, came out of his limitations in his childhood. He swung into action on seeing deprived children, cows being sent to slaughter house and the spread of mass deforestation.

One needs a compelling reason to undertake an act of social justice for which he needs to rope in friends and family. One also needs leadership capability to be secular and draw support from multiple groups. The objective must be to do good work for impacting the lives of children rather than being parochial or prejudiced about social and economic reforms. Can you doubt that the world around us would be made better as murali continues to succeed in his activities and as more such people come into the act?

Footnote:

Murali prefers to write his name as murali.

CHAPTER 14

Befriending nature:
Arun Krishnamurthy,
Founder, Environmentalist Foundation of India

Introduction: If someone were to find a dream job with a dream company when he is aged less than 20, it is natural to expect him to achieve exponential career growth and in his later years, possibly enter the record books for being among the youngest CEOs of a function, domain, or support system in business. Obviously, such opportunities do not knock at everyone's door. Here is the story, which could find a place in a fantasy book, of one such rare person. Arun Krishnamurthy had a fairy-tale start in getting a job at the age of 19 years but quit it in his early 20s. Why Arun sacrificed his high-paying career in an MNC for a social cause would make any one wonder just what his trigger and ambition in life are!

Early days: Arun Krishnamurthy was born in a suburb called Mudichur near Tambaram on the outskirts of Chennai. His house was located in a serene, scenic area surrounded by lush green and a lake near his home. He used to see lots of frogs and snakes, and used to wonder why the snakes ate the frogs! As a child, however, he did not realize that nature has its own way of organizing the food chain for species' subsistence. He did think that unless nature is nurtured and maintained, future generations might suffer.

His schooling also helped him to develop his interest in environment and science. He studied at Good Earth, an institution supported by the Jiddu Krishnamurthy Trust. He commuted nearly 20 km to school every day. He understood the philosophy of Good Earth. Officials at "The School" were specific that he should do what he enjoyed doing. More important, his father shared that sentiment!

Even in the early days of his life, Arun had learnt two important lessons. The first lesson, in two parts, was about the importance of money and the need for frugality. His father made sure everyone at home understood the need to manage personal finance efficiently and appreciated the income and expenditure aspects of family finance. When he was a student in the fourth grade, Arun clearly understood what it meant to build a home with a loan and how much it mattered to repay the loan on time. This taught him frugality and an appreciation of the value of money.

His second big lesson, in three parts, was about hard work, the application of common sense and the development of survival skills. This lesson again came from the family. His father used to work as a General Insurance Development Officer, which meant the harder he worked the more business he achieved. His mother was a PhD in education. She always spoke of making education reforms purposeful. Their natural traits enabled his parents to earn better income by connecting well with people and incidentally, making a social impact.

As he grew to become a youth, Arun imbibed much of his parents' characteristic. His interests in science and nature made him aspire to become a cardiologist. You may consider it the hand of god or a quirk of destiny that Arun landed up at the Madras Christian College, seeking admission to a Bachelor of Science course in microbiology.

This college is located on 360 acres of green lush plants and trees, almost like a forest! The large stretches of greenery gave Arun a lot of inspiration. Further, the college had a very liberal learning system that impacted hard on its students and groomed their leadership skills. Arun was one of those students who could be nurtured to their fullest potential.

Obviously, things were not entirely without conflict for a middle-class boy, however bright and aspiring he was.

Leadership grooming: In his second year at the college, Arun started working on a number of initiatives that helped groom him as a leader. He was pained to see college gutters filled with dried leaves and other garbage. This led to water stagnation, mosquito breeding and adverse effects on the surroundings. He mobilized the support of 14 boys and 36 girls and conveyed his desire to clean up the college campus to the institute's authorities.

Even for a college that had been through all sorts of experiences over a long history, this approach sounded very encouraging to the administrators. They alerted Arun that he was considering what could be a daunting task, considering the effort required to deal with the ground realities of an abundance of wild brush growth, microorganisms and reptiles. The college followed democratic processes. The Principal (Administrative Head of the college) used to preside over sessions called 'An Evening with Tea' with groups of students to discuss new policies and initiatives. Arun was given an opportunity to present his idea about cleaning up the college, and was permitted to go ahead. This was the first environmental clean-up effort handled by him. It gave him the confidence to conceive of larger initiatives for the cause of environment and society.

While at the college, he also used to volunteer at Vandalur Zoo. Being an animal lover, he used to visit the zoo frequently. He was often annoyed by the insensitivity of visitors who failed to appreciate the pain of restricted animals! On one such trip, he found himself highly disturbed, and desired to plunge into action on a project for educating visitors. For a period of eight weeks from that point in time, he conducted a project at the zoo on Sundays, between 11 am to 3 pm, talking to people about how to befriend animals and derive safe and true enjoyment from their trips to the zoo.

Trigger: As he was about to complete his graduation, he got a dream offer from Google India in the area of campaign management.

This gave him huge financial independence at less than 20 years of age. However, he had to move out of Chennai and relocate to Hyderabad. He carried his nature-friendly approach to life to Hyderabad, where he set about exploring his new life.

His love for nature and his experience in handling environmental projects while at college created an urge in Arun to do work that would have a larger impact on social activities. He became interested in restoring lakes while working for Google in Hyderabad. The first lake he initiated a clean-up of in May 2008 was Gurunadham Cheruvu located at Miyapur, Hyderabad. He lived in the Vengal Rao Nagar of Hyderabad and was pained to see the badly neglected Gurunadham Cheruvu Lake in that same area. During one of his cycling trips saw the lake and decided to clean the lake. He spoke to some of his friends and colleagues and informed them of what he had done while at college. A few of them responded positively, but it was not adequate for such a huge task. Arun went on a door-to-door campaign requesting people to join the movement for cleaning up the lake. He targeted children in the age group 10-16 years. He felt that they would bring more enthusiasm and energy to such projects. Grown up people do not unlearn their set attitudes fast and thus, are reluctant to take up simple acts for the benefit of society. He got permission and support from the local government to clean the lake. He had very simple principles, like providing tool, equipment and basic sanitation for all volunteers, including children, who participated in the cleaning up of the lake. No other money was spent. Further, no one, except the organizers, could take photographs for publicity. The project worked wonders!

This experience taught him the lesson that resources, mainly manpower, are the key to successful implementation of projects. He understood that the true game changer in community work is appropriate personnel who volunteer to give time, energy and passion for such work. Even children doing voluntary service under able leadership can help to clean up water bodies and release reptiles belonging to those water bodies back, ensuring survival of the environment. Arun strongly believes that every environment has its own species and organisms that have been thriving there for generations. Nurturing them is critical for environmental survival and for balancing of human interests with those of nature.

Resolve to pursue passion: The second project undertaken by Arun was "Lakshmi Pushkaram" in Chennai in 2009. After Gurunatham Cheruvu, Arun decided to give up his job and come back to Chennai. He thought that by staying closer to home, he could contribute better to social causes. However, his friends thought that giving up a fancy job to pursue his passion might not be the right thing, considering his long-term interests. Arun listened to his heart more than to his mind! Arun says, "Quitting Google in 2010 was a tough decision. They were wonderful employers. But I felt I was slipping into a comfort zone. A full-time job left me little free time to follow my true passion".

He volunteered and ran the Roots & Shoots (R & S), India, program for Dr. Goodall. R & S belongs to the Jane Goodall Institute, under Dr. Jane Goodall, a British primatologist and his mentor. This is more because of a strong emotional attachment he had with Goodall. One of Arun's most prized possessions is a diary that he has maintained since he was in the fourth grade. At that time, his mentor had written a few words in the diary during a visit to India. Goodall inspired him to become a full-time environmentalist.

The major project that he took on was to restore Kilkattalai Lake. This had to be done in several phases: first, the natural habitat and pollutants had to be mapped; garbage had to be cleared; silt had to be removed; and the lake's periphery to be strengthened. This last phase involved reintroduction of native aquatic species and plants. Getting all this done by an individual and a team of volunteers was a major challenge then. It is interesting to learn how Arun managed everything.

Challenges: In 2011, he founded his own NGO, the Environmentalist Foundation of India (EFI), in Chennai. While primarily active in three Indian cities, namely Hyderabad, Chennai and Delhi. one of EFI's most exciting programs is the Lake Biodiversity Restoration Project, which has so far cleaned up 12 lakes across India.

With Kilkattalai Lake, the first challenge was in organizing the required manpower. It was clear that Arun had to use school and college children as his primary manpower resource. The clean-up team consisted of around 900 volunteers, recruited through school programs and street theatre for practical conservation work. Most of them were aged below 20, and had received training from him. He actively mobilized this support direct contact, networking through social media and a number of innovative programs to reach out to students. Many of these students and their parents saw him as a hero. Moreover, these engagements were on holidays and inculcated a sense of social awareness in the children. Hence, parents encouraged their children and often visited the work sites themselves. Arun initiated and experienced this model of engagement, and is now able to use it repeatedly to propel his work in a big way.

The second challenge was getting government department permissions. The initial task was to strengthen the lake's embankments with the support of the government's Public Works Department. Then came removal of the garbage. Generally, Arun found the government departments very friendly and helpful. One needs to work alongside local interest groups to ensure smooth sailing of the projects. This was also the case with the support of government officials.

The third challenge was in funding projects. Initially, Arun used funds he got from Google India. His enthusiasm fetched him the first place in the Google Alumni Impact Awards, which gave him a cash prize of $15,000. This helped him to boost the activities of the EFI. He does not aggressively solicit funding from sponsors, as he feels that his main resources are the people, who are volunteers, at least for now. To meet the rest of the expenses incurred in each intervention, there were sponsors who provide support on request.

Challenge number four was sparing the time that was needed to be devoted. His work was a continuous engagement. He works as a consultant in a communications outfit. From his earnings there, he pumps in 40%-50% to his projects. EFI gets his full-time attention along with his professional work. Though managing both is a demanding exercise, Arun has so far been able to handle it without much difficulty.

In spite of the above constraints, Arun has now expanded his activities. There are about 18 conservation projects, such as cleaning lakes, sparrow reintroduction and herbs restoration, which are handled by him through EFI. The Tamil Nadu Forest Department, the Andhra Pradesh Forest Department and the Delhi State Government have supported the organization's initiatives. Arun taps into the potential of school students and young adults to champion environment causes, and has conducted over 100 school programs in Chennai, Delhi, Hyderabad, Lucknow and Vizag.

Family support: Arun's parents have encouraged him from childhood to choose to work where his heart is. Their hard work, frugality and humbleness have strongly influenced him. Furthermore, his parents thought of him as a sensitive but at the same time objective person, with a no-nonsense attitude when he pursues his dream. Though a sketchy mention has been made, the role of Arun's friends in his path towards becoming an environmentalist is important and needs appreciation.

Conclusion: It is not easy to give up an opportunity to grow in the corporate world to becoming part of a high-level management echelon, especially when the opportunity comes with the advantage of an early start to the career. However, a strong desire to do something a person is passionate about, and the willingness to forgo a potentially rewarding corporate career to impact neighborhoods along with like-minded youth makes for rather brave and revolutionary thinking. Just imagine the environmental benefit to the world if only we had more leaders like Arun pursuing their passion.

CHAPTER 15

Zeal for timely and pure blood for needy:
R.Rajkumar, Blood Donation Campaigner

When you consider the number of accidents and the proliferation of diseases and other medical emergencies requiring surgical interventions that happen around us daily, you may well wonder how one would ensure adequate supply of blood merely through voluntary donations. We all know blood is the most vital fluid in the human body. It is perishable, and stocks of blood cannot be stored for long. Most of us know that the average human body needs five to six liters of blood for healthy survival. Blood is composed of plasma and several other kinds of cells. The average common man seldom understands the importance of blood transfusion and blood bank service until he himself faces a medical emergency that necessitates blood for someone near and dear. While many of us appreciate that blood is an essential medical inventory, we are happy to leave the responsibility for making blood available when needed to hospitals.

I must admit my own inability for a long time to understand the realities of medical blood requirements. I always wondered about the great service rendered by international organizations like the Red Cross, by blood banks and by hospitals. I felt that donating blood was the work of a few souls bent upon benevolence to society. It was foolhardy to relate blood donations to largeness of heart without understanding that there is an ongoing, imperative need for blood, and that systematic work, often in terms of compelling surgical interventions, is required to ensure the survival of people involved in critical accidents. The most unfortunate are those who suffer from blood-related disease such as *thalassemia*. It is worth noting that even in the most advanced countries, only about 5% of the people donate blood; their repeat donations enable the demand for blood to be met.

It was in this context, given the high importance of voluntary blood donations and the role of organizations, that I came across Rajkumar, who had been performing this service with passion and commitment.

Rajkumar first donated blood when he was part of the NSS at his college. It so happened that the college requested more volunteers to donate blood because it was short by six students to top the list of Madurai colleges donating blood. This motivated Rajkumar to come forward to donate himself and also canvass his fellow students successfully to donate, steering his college to the top position among its peers. He got another 21 students to donate. According to Rajkumar, "NSS was a great motivator for me to align myself in service, especially in the area of blood donations".

There were other factors also that drove him to this level of service. One was the upbringing he had received in his family. His parents had encouraged him from childhood to serve the community and be associated with good work for common causes. He used to listen to a number of motivating incidents when his parents and relatives had been involved in social activities, and the same imbibed the spirit himself.

Another trigger to serve with distinction was his association with Shanthi Ranganathan, the founding Director and Honorary Secretary of the Chennai-based T.T. Krishnamachari Clinical Research Foundation

(T.T.K. Hospital). He enjoyed the privilege of associating with her in his early days of work, and her relentless work on social issues motivated him. He keenly observed her planning, time management and commitment to excellence in her services to society, and he internalized these qualities.

Even when he was young, Rajkumar believed that to save lives you don't need a medical degree, though having one is, of course, an asset. One can save lives through activities such as blood and organ donation. The proper orientation toward timely critical support in saving a life is what is more important.

According to Rajkumar, the top management where he worked played a critical role in shaping his personality and service orientation. After completing his post graduation in commerce in the late 1970s, Rajkumar joined the Indian Bank. He has worked there for three decades, primarily based in Chennai. It would have a normal approach for someone from the middle class to pursue a banking career, work on the challenges of moving up the hierarchy and retiring from a senior position.

Rajkumar pursued a different ambition while at the bank. He heard a call of conscience to serve society by creating a network for voluntary blood donation. He joined the bank at a time when there were mass recruitments to the bank and thus, had a large peer group. Being charismatic, Rajkumar was able to establish quick personal links with people. In 1979, he started actively pursuing his prime interest in promoting blood donation, at his place of work. He emerged as a leader, and was influential among the youth in the bank, who happily came forward to donate blood. It is interesting to note here that he has organized about 1,055 blood donation events, 51% in coordination with his employer, Indian Bank, and the remaining 49% through other partnerships. This required phenomenal effort and drive. The number of donors he has arranged is about 105,000, of which 17,000 were on emergency calls. If one assumes one emergency call a day, the total runs to 46 man-years of blood donating effort. That is a tall order to achieve, indeed.

The functioning links between donation camps and emergencies are quite interesting. As blood cannot be stocked for long periods, there must be good estimation of requirements, coordination and management of donors. The capacities of recipient stock centers and utilization are critical. Ranking above everything else in importance is the need to attend to emergency calls for blood. Managing a blood supply network with efficiency requires a high level of understanding of donors and their situations. It was not through any scheduling program or sophisticated modeling that Rajkumar managed his efforts. Sheer dedication, commitment and charisma, along with the largesse of donors, helped him achieve this.

A normal, healthy human can give blood once in two months. To be a leader, action is more important rather than strategizing and making promises. It is essential for a leader to lead by example, by donating blood himself in voluntary groups and so drive others to emulate him. Rajkumar has donated blood more than 60 times, in spite of his busy schedules and his commitment to building up this voluntary movement. He has demonstrated the highest quality of leadership, and set an example for others to follow.

National Aids Control Organisation, of which Rajkumar is a member, states that at any time, demand for blood in terms of number of units is equivalent to 1.1% of the population in any urban agglomeration or in any other place in India. By these statistics, demand in India would be around 1.3 crore units, whereas less than one crore units are donated *voluntarily*. The rest of the requirement is left to 2,700 blood banks, both in the government and NGO sectors, to meet. According to one statistic, there are 67 countries where demand for blood is met a hundred percent by voluntary donations. It is important that people understand the importance of voluntary donations and measure up to the demand. According to Rajkumar, "blood cells die every 120 days and are replaced by new cells. The physiology of the human body is supportive of blood donations, but people seldom realize this."

It is worth noting Rajkumar's special interest in thalassaemic children. He is the founder of the Thalassaemic Society of Tamil Nadu. Thalassemia is an inherited hematological disorder caused by defects in the synthesis of one or more of the hemoglobin (Hb) chains. Hb is the protein in red blood cells that carries oxygen. Hence, thalassemia patients suffer from anemia and iron deficiency. Thalassemia can cause significant complications, including pneumonia, iron overload, bone deformities and cardiovascular illness. One of the treatments is frequent blood transfusions. The Association of Voluntary Blood Donors founded by Rajkumar donates blood from 50,000 donors every year. At present, his organization is supporting 208 children to get free blood transfusion every month. These are all tall achievements by a person who has a modest approach to service.

It must be noted that thalassemia is more prevalent in certain regions of India, especially among low-income groups. It is a hereditary condition, and the corrective process is difficult and expensive. Management of the condition through blood transfusions is an important element of treatment. Rajkumar was ahead of his times in pursuing the goal of assisting thalassemia patients by supporting availability of blood through his network. It took phenomenal initiative to be a pioneer and a founder of a society for helping affected children. To understand this better, one must observe the pains that a family with a thalassaemic member undergoes as they swing between hope and despair. Every transfusion of blood is a harbinger of hope for survival. Rajkumar fully understands the pain felt by victims and their families, and provides support to enable affected children to live a little more in a better frame of mind and spirit. While the common man may see this as the "hand of God" or as a "matter of luck", Rajkumar sees things through a different window. Committing to even the remotest chances of success may not always be prudent in life, but that assurance is what a person looks forward to when fighting against severe odds. We all realize this truth only when something adverse happens to our own kin. The visionary Rajkumar saw this as a social problem and mustered support to fight it. He demonstrates his sincerity in action. He has adopted seven children afflicted with thalassemia. This is selflessness of the highest order, requiring humongous courage to act when there are so many other commitments in life. That is the quality social leadership calls for!

Behind this successful man there are a few support systems. I need to mention for the benefit of those who may want to emulate him. His immediate family perfectly understands his aspirations and drive, and acknowledges the happiness it gives because of his service to society. He gives his family whatever time is left over after he meets his priorities and commitments to blood donations and other social activities. He gets equally strong support from his employer, Indian Bank. While Rajkumar works hard at his official duties, and enjoys excellent relations with the customers of the bank, he has become the ambassador of the bank in many senses. The bank and its employees stand firm with him in fulfilling his call of conscience to serve the needy the best way he can. A third factor is his network of friends, who see Rajkumar as an embodiment of love for fellow humans. They consider him a perfect person in fulfilling commitments based on trust and faith. The strength of this network can be realized by studying a recent incident when there was an SOS call to him from a patient in New Thippasumudra, Bangalore, who was about to undergo an emergency operation. Rajkumar connected with someone at Bangalore and the demand for blood was fulfilled in 30 minutes. Such is the power of networking, where a couple of phone calls and the glad support of well-intended people saved a life.

It is amazing that Rajkumar has sustained his initiative for three decades!

Rajkumar is a compulsive, aggressive communicator capable of encouraging friends and colleagues to support his mission by using his oratory skills. He has presented papers in over 65 national and international forums and has given a number of radio talks. He has been involved in different levels of voluntary service, and has been a member of notable institutions such as the Red Cross and the State Blood Transfusion Council. Incidentally, leadership in social activities is recognized and motivated through awards! He has received about 119 awards, some of them the most prestigious recognition for organizing the highest number of blood donors in the state by the government of Tamil Nadu. Such motivation leads to larger initiatives. He proposes to set up a model blood bank exclusively run by voluntary blood donors in association with an NGO, aiming to provide blood to all needy patients at all times. Furthermore, he intends to open a dementia and Alzheimer care centre to help people affected with these diseases.

We can conclude that for someone to carry on the task of organizing donations blood consistently over three decades, thereby serving the truly needy, requires a strong will, commitment, energy and the ability to keep one's head in the right place without bias and without getting tempted by the materialistic aspects of life. Remember that in Rajkumar's case all this was done while he was working full time with a leading bank and leading a normal family life. Rajkumar makes me feel that champions are driven by altruistic goals and excellent operational capabilities, and thereby, make a difference to society. For such people, awards, recognition and market valuations are incidentals and not the driving goals of life.

Rajkumar's life ambitions are to ensure that no one dies for want of blood and that Tamil Nadu is free of thalassemia within a decade. Well, for many this ambition it is quixotic! To me, it sounds bold and courageous. When Dr. V. Kurien thought India should lead in dairy production and launched the white revolution with the support of the World Bank, it would have sounded like an over-ambitious dream to most. One must consider the vision of Rajkumar, which he has passionately built up over three decades. This must be encouraged and supported by all, especially by youth. If all of us identify the problems of society and are willing to act on eradicating them with commitment, like Rajkumar, we would take the world infinitely far!

CHAPTER 16

A journey in life with an experience of love and oneness in abundance: Dr. B.Sailakshmi, Founder, Ekam Foundation

ntroduction: When someone is born to a family of doctors, we almost take it for granted that person will also become a doctor. More importantly, that person may either pursue a roaring practice or dedicate him or herself to working in a community or public health system to serve the poor. Rarely does one come across a highly qualified doctor giving up her medical practice to pursue her inner interest in setting up appropriate administrations and systems for providing health care to newborn children and babies whose parents cannot afford intensive care to save their children from threatening conditions. Dr. Sailakshmi Balijepalli (Sai), moved by experiences with infants dying for want of medical care, decided to dedicate her life to eliminating this scourge.

Early days: Dr. Sai was born into a family of doctors. Both of her parents had excellent practices. Sai's sister also pursued medicine and became a cardiologist. In fact, her sister is Sai's motivator, friend and mentor in all her activities. Sai has not just adopted any religious tenet but is creating a social movement and derives a lot of motivation from her family.

When she was young, Sai also dreamed of becoming a doctor. She did her entire schooling at Keyes High School for Girls, Secunderabad, between 1977 and 1989. Between 1989 and 1991, she attended St. Francis College for Women, Secunderabad, for a two years' intermediate course in biology, physics and chemistry. In 1992, she joined the Gandhi Medical College, Hyderabad, and completed her Bachelor of Medicine & Bachelor of Surgery, Medicine courses in 1997. She did her internship in the period 1997-1998. She did her postdoctoral Diploma in Child Health in 1999-2000 at a premier institute in Hyderabad. She further did her postdoctoral course for the Diploma of National Board in Pediatrics between 2001 and 2003. Her educational background reflects her scholastic brilliance all through her academic life and shows how keen she was on pediatrics. The obvious question that arises is: what has she been achieving with her academic excellence and her quest for impeachable knowledge on pediatric medical care?

Trigger and impacts: Sai's parents were highly spiritual even as they were busy with their profession. Listening to religious discourses, talks on moral lessons from epics, divine songs and prayers, and studying art were the norm of life. She grew up understanding the value of service and kept asking questions about the purpose of the soul from childhood. She always felt that God has created every human with a purpose, and one's ultimate calling is to identify that purpose and work towards fulfilling it. As a kid, she loved philosophy and the question, "what am I?" jaunted her a lot.

Her sister constantly nudged her to pursue her education with excellence and made her dream of saving lives by becoming a doctor. She insisted that Sai should not work for money, but should put service ahead of money.

Sai says, "maybe our vision of freedom of life to every child born is a very ambitious one". Further, she quotes an unknown author: "There are infinite imaginative possibilities when we allow freedom to go beyond our perceived limits. If we can dream it, we can build it. Life through unconditional love is a wondrous adventure that excites the very core of our being and lights our path with delight".

Her path was not as easy as one may think. Though there were quite a few transformations, she always had the liberty given by her parents to pursue whatever she wanted as long as she held on to her dignity and truthfulness. Furthermore, they preferred that she use her strengths, her knowledge of medicines, to succeed in her chosen path in life.

Sai was instinctive in her early stages. She was a person who felt the compulsion to serve the needy, however demanding that service was on her in terms of time and other resources. Two instances in her life vouch for her commitment.

The first instance came about when a major earthquake hit the state of Gujarat on January 26, 2001. It killed 20,000 people, injured another 167,000 and left about 400,000 homeless. Sai left for relief work, missing her post-graduate entrance examinations.

The second instance was when she was working in Chennai. On August 18, 2008, Bihar experienced one of the most disastrous floods in its history. A breach in the Kosi embankment near the Indo-Nepal border inundated large tracts of land and washed away many populous villages. The flood affected over 2.3 million people in the northern part of Bihar. Sai jumped at the opportunity to do relief work. Here, she met Ashoka Fellow Anshu Gupta, who became her mentor and later, a board member of Ekam, the foundation she established.

The real trigger that propelled her into social service could have been her first patient when she was doing her internship in the government hospital. Kulsumbi, the patient, was in her mid-thirties. She was in a precarious condition and could not afford treatment at a private hospital. She required some surgical interventions. Just as a challenge, Sai's teacher encouraged her to take the case over and do whatever she could. Sai operated on the woman and resorted to "beg and borrow" medicines and surgical and clinical accessories to treat her. The patient responded, but Sai's term ended, and she was posted to a different assignment. Her mind lingered around the woman she had treated, and the question she kept asking herself was "why does not God help such people?" It was a typical case of lack of money power making death laugh at a critical patient in a general hospital, where the support systems are inadequate or underprepared or both.

After a few weeks, she visited the ward and found that the patient got her discharged and left. However, no address was available for her. Though Sai felt relieved that the woman was cured, she was uncomfortable because of her inability to understand patient recovery. In a twist of destiny, the woman reappeared after a couple of months. She mentioned to Sai that she had lost hopes of survival before Sai's intervention made it possible. It is impossible to believe that an intern can leave such an impact on a patient! However, Sai took the case seriously, and decided her future was in providing intensive care for those who could not afford it.

Opportunities and challenges: Sai was frustrated with the inadequacies of the health care available in India. She witnessed the number of children who were becoming victims of the inefficiencies of the system, and saw doctors increasingly accepting these deaths as a routine problem. Often, she observed that the intensive care unit (ICU) had limitations. Children were often admitted to the ICU a little too late, and more important, many parents of the patients could not make firm decisions on whether and how much to spend on the afflicted child. They had other children, and they were severely limited by their inability to afford the ICU facility.

These observations and internal reluctance to submit tamely to the existing situation pushed her to search for solutions. Initially, she assumed the role of a proactive doctor who visited orphanages around her hospital to identify, refer and treat sick children.

Later, to achieve large-scale impact, she created a project that connected private doctors to orphanages around their hospitals. To quote her, "It started in 2006 as a community pediatric health project of

Mehta children's Hospital, where I was working as a junior consultant in the neonatal ICU. We initially tied up with 60 pediatricians who were friends, colleagues and teachers, and matched them to 60 orphanages based on their location. We asked them to take up ownership for health care of the children attached to their orphanage".

Initially everyone was enthusiastic, but because of busy schedules, they were not able to visit the orphanages regularly. However, they were willing to see all the children referred to them free of cost. Accordingly, we started a nodal clinic model such that these children would be referred to the nearest pediatrician.

It was still a bit of a challenge to stay within a medical and hospital system and deliver effectively on this model. Sai decided to improve the model's efficiency. She quit her job and started Ekam Foundation.

In 2009, she registered Ekam Foundation as a not-for-profit organization. As the most vulnerable children came from adoption agencies, she started by training caretakers to identify sick children in time, provide emergency care and improves nutrition as needed. Later, she expanded her operations to government schools, where most orphaned children studied.

Eventually, this network covered 80,000 children in Chennai. After witnessing the need for effective follow-up on treatment, she also started school health clubs. The teachers found this important initiative to be rewarding because it brought about observably improved productivity in the children. Sai's idea of involving diverse stakeholders for health, like local political and social officials in district health committees, has emerged from the experience with school health clubs. Children were often transferred to government hospitals when their families had no resources to pay. Closing the loop, Dr. Sai realized she needed to go back to working within the government system as with smaller investments, one could achieve a greater impact.

Connecting with friends and well-wishers: She approached one of her friends namely Prasanna, who takes care of the Confederation of Indian Organisations for service and Advocacy (CIOSA), an arm of MaFoi to support activities through Ekam Foundation. MaFoi promoters Mr. K. Pandia Rajan and Latha Rajan became trustees of Ekam Foundations. Other eminent professionals also help Sai in setting the right vision for Ekam Foundation. Sai is clear that one individual cannot do full justice to a good cause. She feels she needs to scale operations to reflect practical needs and establish a proper system.

Furthermore, true to her instincts, she believes that a good medical professional may not be the best administrator most of the times, though there could be exceptions. She felt that there is a void when it comes to administration in public health systems. She thought she would focus more on filling in the void.

The following achievements highlight her daunting spirit and ambition to stretch her network as wide as possible for better reach:

She networked with almost 51 hospitals and 150 pediatricians to take care of all referrals after screening the children. All these hospitals admit the children under subsidies and credit facilities given to Ekam Foundation.

After she started working with ICH, Egmore, Chennai, Sai tied up with other government hospitals like those in Chengalpet and Virudhunagar and Madurai's Rajaji Hospital.

In October 2010, Ekam received official permission from the National Rural Health Mission to appoint 234 nurses in all 37 medical college hospitals and district headquarter hospitals in the state and monitor all 41 sick newborn care units established in the state for reducing the neonatal mortality rate as part of a public-private partnership initiative.

She has constantly been working with this group on advocacy as well as on action in emergencies. She has now started working in Mumbai on a similar project. It is amazing to find her so involved in saving the lives of children. Sai says, "I think it is the collective responsibility of all of us to see that no child is denied access to the needs that help the child survive. This is freedom of life!" She also believes that she supports government hospitals and does not compete with them, as her target segment is poor children who cannot afford private care.

Visionary Thinking: Sai became cognizant of that the fact that mortality was highest among younger children and poor children who did not go to school. Seeking direct reach to migrant workers and communities in slums, she started community-based work on preventive neonatal and childcare. Ekam also created a community children's insurance scheme. Though her heart beats for these schemes, her mind faces the challenges of maintaining the financial sustainability of these efforts.

She is trying to tie up funding arrangements with government schemes, international agencies and private partnerships. Sai happily mentions the number of individual donors who support her activity. Going forward, she wants to set up excellent operational standards for her project, with clear transparency and objectivity. The project trustees also share her ideas.

Conclusion: India is a country where it is common for professionals to groom their children to take up the same professions, join them in their practice and create family-run medical institutions. In the case of Sai, we find a scholastic doctor who quit her medical practice to establish an administrative set up for providing ICU services to poor children and thus reduce infant mortality in the country. It is not that just a development indicator which hurts her! Her humanity makes her take it as a "call of the soul". Her reading of Ramakrishna and Vivekananda's works was so intense and forceful that she decided to set an example of their preaching by her practice. It is not that who said what that matters, but who does what! It is the understanding of the meaning of kindness to society and especially to poor children. It is dedicating life to work based on that understanding that matters. One can shy away from normal life by moving to religious groups to serve as a dedicated member. One can also opt to serve in a limited capacity when one has large financial support. Sai chose to show courage by being different and accepting the challenges of administering and bringing energy to build an organization around a humane cause. So many more of the world's children would be enabled to lead a normal, healthy life if we had just a few more Sais around us.

CHAPTER 17

Friends becoming saviors:
Khasim Shareef, Founder, Friends2support.org

Introduction: The most common complaint we would hear from people born in the more remote villages of India is the lack of schools and other educational infrastructure that would help people study and progress in life. Many of these people have fought this shortcoming by taking hours to travel long distances to obtain high school education. Once they are through high school, they take support from some source or the other to graduate from a college in a nearby town. Finally, the more persevering of such people end up becoming more average citizens of urban areas and focusing on building their lives. The rarest of them progress further by excelling in both their education and their first job. Some of them then demonstrate their drive by managing to go abroad, looking for greener pastures. This last phase is more common among people working in the information technology industry or in academics and research. We rarely hear of instances of someone remarkable enough to give up life on foreign soil to return to their home country with ambitions of serving the larger community. Khasim Shareef is one such extraordinary human; he returned to India to balance the demands of his professional life with the demands imposed by the exemplary work he does in the social sector, work that touches millions of Indians. In this chapter, we try to capture his trigger, drive and passion to make the world better for everyone.

Early days: Shareef comes from a humble rural background in India. He was born and reared in Inumella, a village in Guntur district of Andhra Pradesh. Like so many other Indian villages, this village did not even have a high school until 1997. To quote Shareef about the infrastructure of this village, "I remember my village had only two bus connections to the nearest town: one in the morning and the second in the evening." In all honesty, though, one must consider Shareef to have been better off when compared to other numerous rural Indians who have to walk miles barefooted to get to a bus route or even to a school.

Shareef's father was a school teacher in his village. One can only try to imagine how difficult it must have been for the family of a school teacher in such a remote place to make ends meet. Shareef, the youngest of three sons, has one sister. He did his schooling till the seventh grade in his father's school, which was the only school in not only this village, but also over an area of a few more hamlets in the vicinity. Students who wanted to pursue further education had to do so in a school in the nearest town. Like everyone else in his village, Shareef went to the nearest town, Narasaraopet, 35 km from his village, to obtain high school education (grades eight to ten). In fact, he went on to complete his post-graduation from the same town, commuting every day from his home at the village. Travelling such a distance over the village and state roads and highways of India is not easy. The average speed for a public vehicle is less than 20 kms per hour. Shareef used to leave home by 7 a.m. and return at around 7 p.m. on a normal day. Life used to be even tougher during the monsoon, as the bus service became unreliable because of poor road conditions. This kind of demanding experience prodded Shareef and his family into building up their spirits and resolving to fight all odds, so they could progress on to a life of meaningful achievement.

When talking about his interests, Shareef says, "From my childhood, I was very interested in drawing. So I decided to go in for a career in the same field." Like most middle-class non-metro Indians, Shareef's awareness of career opportunities was limited. Similarly, Shareef did not know what career opportunities there were in the field of drawing. The normal tendency in such a situation is to look for guidance from members of the nucleus family. In the case of Shareef, all of his siblings, who preferred government jobs, completed their B.Ed. courses and ended up as teachers. This trend ran in the family because their father motivated them. Furthermore, the typical approach of poor rural Indians is to look for a secured future in government service, and since teaching was seen as a noble profession, they were happy. However, Shareef thought that he could take positional advantage of being the youngest in the family and pursue a technical skill-based course to get into the IT sector. Consequently, he moved to Hyderabad and earned his Advanced Diploma in Multimedia from a leading learning centre.

Tough times and break through:

Shareef had to live in difficult circumstances while and immediately after doing this course. He hardly had any money. To quote him: "After completing my course in multimedia, I tried for a job. I applied at a number of companies. Sometimes, I used to walk 20 km just to attend an interview. This was because I did not even have Rs. 5 for a bus ticket. The year 2003 was a memorable year in my life, as I was appointed as a trainee designer by a knowledge management company at Hyderabad. When I got the offer letter specifying a salary of Rs. 5000 per month from the company, I felt like I had won everything I wanted in my life."

Working for that knowledge management company allowed Shareef to enjoy a much more comfortable lifestyle. He made friends and achieved social respect. He also developed the desire to be successful. He understood the power of online communities and decided that he must use this power for a social good. He knew facilities for education in the rural sector were suffering due to lack of infrastructure. He felt that he would find it difficult as an individual to harness technology efficiently to supplement school education facilities in villages. He was impressed, however, by the many corporate initiatives that had been launched in that domain. He also felt the alternative urge to do something else in the social sector using technology and social groups.

Trigger and drive for F2S (Friends to Support):

Shareef read a number of disturbing news items on unethical blood donation practices. To quote him, "In 2000-01, a heart-rending incident was published in one of the dailies that triggered my idea of setting up a 'F2S' organization. Kids of age 12-15 years, who were playing a cricket match in their neighborhood, were lured by an unauthorized blood bank to donate blood, in exchange for goodies. Later, I read about another incident where rickshaw-pullers were offered alcohol to donate blood. I was surprised to note that one rickshaw-puller went to the blood bank fortnightly to donate pints. These incidents really inspired the thought of improving public awareness of proper and ethical blood donation." Thus, F2S was inspired by the organizational malfunctioning that characterized most blood donation camps. Even hospitals had a casual attitude to blood donation and lacked a systemic approach to this sensitive issue. Although there were innumerable incidents of wrong practices, a few of them that came to Shareef's attention left an indelible mark on him and eventually lead to the foundation of F2S. The one spark that triggered action occurred when a close neighborhood friend succumbed prematurely due to excessive blood loss. Further he mentioned that none of his relatives, friends or neighbors had voluntarily stepped to donate to save the life. According to Shareef, people hesitated to help because of fear of giving blood; they lacked adequate knowledge of relevant aspects of blood donation and its impact on healthy living. "When I thought over these incidents, I felt sad more than enraged. I felt the real cause behind such incidents was nothing but lack of awareness among common people of the value of timely blood donations. This lack of knowledge led to victimization of people who would otherwise have been eager donors."

Therefore, Shareef launched F2S as a vehicle not only to create a pool of donors but also to raise awareness among common people on how to donate for a good cause without being exploited or lured.

Friendstosupport (F2S) is a website on which potential blood donors from all over the country can voluntarily register, while those in need of donors can find them very easily. "We wanted to make the common man realize that there are some things in this world for which he doesn't have to fight, at least, not anymore. This is why Friendstosupport was started." The website allows any person to register and volunteer to be a blood donor. Those in need of blood can choose the city, the required blood group and the kind of donor best suited for them.

Supreme sense of commitment:

While working in the knowledge management company, Shareef started the Friends2support.org website. Four childhood friends, Naveen Reddy, Koteswararao S., Phani Kethamakka and Murali Krishna from Narasaraopet, Guntur district, Andhra Pradesh, joined Shareef as the cofounders of Friendstosupport.org, a non-profit blood donation organization (networked through website) that they launched on November 14, 2005. It is interesting to note how these five inexperienced friends united under the leadership of Shareef to bring about this initiative. They lacked the sophistication of urban education and rich family backgrounds, and had no exposure to business. They only had the commitment to do good to society with whatever they could command in terms of resources and knowledge. Now, almost 10 years after the launch of this foundation, one can observe the power of social media. In 2005, however, there were hardly any instances where friends got together to create an enterprise for social good using the power of Internet. That was the sense of commitment Shareef and his friends demonstrated. Shareef's later actions will show that this first action was not an accident or the result of a rush of blood to the head.

After working in the knowledge management company for five years, Shareef got an opportunity to go to the UK on deputation by a mid-size IT company. To quote Shareef, "After one year in the UK, I thought that apart from the money I was earning, nothing was there for me in life abroad. Moreover, I felt that I couldn't properly monitor Friends2support.org's work from outside India. So I came back to India to focus more on my organization".

He joined another private company in Hyderabad as a design manager. He focused both on his profession and the F2S activities. For someone from a poor background to have raised enough in life to get a job abroad and then sacrifice that job for a social cause back home is highly commendable. These decisions are not easy unless one has a strong vision and a sense of supreme commitment to serve society. When we study these decisions, we discover that for the people making those decisions, monetary considerations alone do not drive career decisions. They learn how to balance their need for money with their urge to contribute to society on their own terms. Such people generally demonstrate developed leadership traits and the ability to leverage resources and teams.

Challenges in taking ahead:

Given today's technology and the ease of access to that technology, it may look easy to create a forum of Internet users as a social group. For Shareef, considering the cause for which he set up F2S, it was almost an insurmountable task. Shareef and the other founders became the first donors. As they persisted, people joined their forum, which thus grew in size. Many of them had to manage their jobs, some of which were in the demanding IT sector. The challenge spurred them to spread the idea. In their spare time, they mailed everyone they knew about the site. The recipients, in turn, spread the word to more people. Shareef and his friends held gatherings and approached people door-to-door, and that was how F2S gained popularity.

According to Shareef, "The real task was to convince people about the soundness of the idea. We faced a lot of discouragement initially.

A thorough research had to be done on the myths and facts of blood donation; the present system of blood donation had to be studied; and relevant data on blood donation had to be obtained with the cooperation of people like medicos. Finding the right persons and convincing them to cooperate was a difficult task. Eight years down the lane, though F2S still faces many challenges, I am glad that people have accepted the idea wholeheartedly and are coming forward to volunteer."

Shareef and his friends work on the principle that "One should donate blood only when the need arises and not for incentives, which are usually given to exploit people who are less informed." The donors on the website have registered with the sole purpose of serving society. They donate blood voluntarily out of goodwill.

F2S has conducted many landmark events, such as bike rallies, walks and signature campaigns for creating awareness, to promote their idea across the country. At all instances the public participated in great numbers.

Shareef has plans for future. He wants to establish a toll-free number across the country that will support all languages. He also plans to concentrate on rural education and start a book donation website. According to him, "Don't you think that as a citizen of a country of 1.2 billion people, it is senseless for a common man to have to *buy* blood, especially when there are lakhs of people who wholeheartedly come forward to donate blood? Any person in need of blood at any place in India should get it within minutes, thereby putting an end to the colossal wastage of valuable blood collected at blood donation camps. This is what we believe in. On that note, F2S chugs on."

Friends2support, which is now accessible in every corner of India, has grown to 115,000 registered volunteer donors in eight years, and has become the world's largest voluntary blood donor database. Shareef and F2S have won a number of awards. Shareef is the winner of the World Summit Youth Award—2013; runner up for the United Nations World Summit Youth Award—2009; mBillionth South Asia Award—2013; nominee for the Nasscom Innovation Honors—2009; and winner of the Manthan Award—2007. F2S features in the Limca Book of Records as

India's largest voluntary blood donor website continuously for the years 2010-2013. F2S also features in the Asia Book of Records for 2012 as Asia's largest voluntary blood donor website and in the India Book of Records for 2012 as the world's largest voluntary blood donor website. F2S won the Andhra Pradesh State Government Award in 2012 and 2013 for its efforts in promoting voluntary blood donation. Though records and awards mean nothing in terms of F2S's efforts and their value to society, Shareef feels that these endorsements make the community closer and stronger.

Family support: For Shareef, his family has been a great motivator and supporter of his dreams. His family members have stood by him through all the actions he took to realize his dreams. As a teacher, his father had imbued him with the spirit of giving and acting beyond his own interest. He also helped Shareef learn to handle the challenging demands of time and limitations of resources. His parents trained Shareef right from his childhood to pursue his ambitions and synchronize his actions to scale up his activities. In addition to the emotional support he received from his siblings, his village and school friends, who grew up in similar conditions, have been great supports for Shareef.

Conclusion: Shareef is a role model for many rural Indian youth to pursue their ambitions for education and involve themselves in social causes using their knowledge and their networks of friends. Instead of lamenting on the failure of prevailing systems, it is far more commendable to seize all opportunities to work to impact society along with one's personal choice of career. Social conditions the world over would be better with more youth taking up approaches like that of Shareef.

CHAPTER 18

Living the belief "service to mankind is one way to realize God!": Dr. R.Balasubramaniam[1], Founder, Swami Vivekananda Youth Mission

ntroduction: At the age of 19, one decides to set up a social organization to serve the poor and the downtrodden, especially in the tribal hamlets of the Western Ghats near Mysore. More so unbelievable because in next couple of years this person graduates to become a doctor from a prestigious medical college in Karnataka with a seat on merit (and the top rank all through the course). A typical medical professional would have aspired to go for post graduation, and set up and pursue a roaring practice in an urban centre. In some cases, one may add the flavor of service through low fees from patients of low-income groups. However, Dr. Balasubramaniam (Balu) chose to commit himself to fulfilling the unfelt needs of tribal people.

I feel difficult to believe that such things happen in India. One always thinks that medial education is expensive and a person needs to be intellectually and economically privileged to become a "doctor". After such ego-boosting success at an young age, the "doctor" needs to be busy 24X7 for 365 days serving people with focus on building up a strong practice, ensuring a reasonable "return on investment" on expensive education and on the infrastructure created for practice. All along, one would hear about successful treatment being credited to the skills of the doctor and adding intangible value to his or her reputation. Failure, on the other hand, is ascribed to "destiny". In such a complex setting, Balu is a nonconformist.

He neither practiced for generating personal wealth (value creation by self and appropriation for self) nor preferred to fly to developed countries to improve his professional credentials and then make wealth there. Actually, one may hear how benevolent are those few doctors who went abroad and came back to serve their country. Our debate is not about personal wealth creation being good or bad. One needs to create wealth. At the same time, society needs professionals who can also address needs that downtrodden people have. We call such professionals champions. Fortunately, India has quite a few of them.

It is more important to note here that Balu has transformed himself from a medical professional in the development sector into a social entrepreneur, and later, into a development leader. He now adorns different positions as a policy analyst, teacher, mentor and a force for change, all with simplicity and humility and a caring attitude towards the poor and those deserving to be served. His conduct over the years has been phenomenal. He has managed an internal transformation that helps him look inward in solving social issues and still be simple and avoid running after recognitions, rewards and the limelight.

Early days: Balu studied in St. Joseph's Indian High School in Bangalore. He comes from a middle-class family and has two siblings. His father taught him the importance of education and his mother taught him the importance of values in life. They are a close-knit family with typical respect for values and beliefs. Education was important. He had frequent occasion to observe his brother studying well and their sister being groomed in a typical South Indian value-based family tradition. He had been competitive, with the determination to excel in his work. He enjoyed playing and competing with classmates. His father always encouraged Balu to be independent and seek high accomplishments in education, as he had suffered for being economically backward. He never wanted his children to suffer in their life. "Coming up" always meant a benchmark with peers in terms of socioeconomic status and moving up. Balu understood such carvings deeply but was not sure whether he had the same need for himself.

Triggers: Balu scored very high marks in the Pre-University examination of Karnataka State and wanted to pursue engineering. Whether through destiny or misfortune, he did not qualify for admission to pursue an education in engineering with the Indian Institutes of Technology. His next expectation was to make it to the Regional Engineering College (now known as National Institute of Engineering) at Suratkal to specialize in computer science. Unfortunately, he did not make it there as well.

To quote Balu,

> disappointed, I tried to settle down by choosing mechanical engineering at BMS Engineering College, Bangalore. I was ragged so badly on the first day that I did not have the courage to go back to the college the next day. My middle class background meant that I could not stay at home nor spend time somewhere else. I had to leave home and do something which did not cost me money but somehow killed time. I set out the next day dreading what was in store for me. As I neared the college, I lost all courage. Thankfully, I noticed the Ramakrishna Ashram close to the college and decided to spend time in the lush green campus. I started going there every day and landed up reading the works of Swami Vivekananda at the library.

Two small books written by Swamiji deserve mention here; they changed my life forever. One was 'His call to the Nation' and the other 'To the Youth of India'. Suddenly there was so much clarity in my mind. I resolved that if I were to get an opportunity to take up medicine, I would go to the villages of India and work for their development as per the call given by Swami Vivekananda in these books.

It was Saturday, 29th of September 1982, when I made a commitment to myself that if I were to get a medical seat, then my life would be dedicated to serving our rural brethren in remote corners of India. The same day, I found a telegram from the Director of Medical Education asking me to join the Mysore Medical College (MMC). It was divine sign clarifying to me my life's mission.

I went to Mysore on the 3rd of October with my father to get myself admitted to MMC. Both of us met the Principal, Dr. Shankar Raj. He told me that no admission was possible until he received the official letter from the DME. I was so devastated that I could not hold back my tears. An elderly person stopped to enquire what the matter was. Hesitatingly and holding back my tears, I explained to him my predicament. He patiently listened to me and then gently asked me not to worry. He told me that he was the Office Superintendent and that all letters would first be received by him. He asked me not lose heart. I suddenly felt that I could not lose faith in myself. Otherwise, what use was reading Swamiji and his works if I could not apply it in my own life!

The letter arrived by the day's registered mail. I got myself admitted. I then felt convinced that I was destined to live my life differently. (http://rbalu.wordpress.com/2009/05/22/4-how-the-seeds-were-sown/)

A couple of incidents and their deep impact on the goal: It was February 1984 when he was posted to the Internal Medicine unit in a hospital at Mysore. One of the patients in the ward was a 44-year-old Brahmin cook from a village who was turning out to be a "difficult case". Since he was not responding to any treatment, the diagnosis was of "idiopathic malignant hypertension" which means that the cause was unknown (idiopathic).

Balu narrates further,

> One early morning, I learnt that the patient had died the previous night. I found his 73-year-old mother (elderly widowed lady) packing up and courtesy demanded that I console her. As I approached her, she burst out crying inconsolably. She had sold half an acre of irrigated land for paying for the costs of treatment of her son, who was the sole earning member. Now she had not only lost her son, but also all hope. I felt small for not understanding so much of her 'social and economic' history.

> I was so numb that I did not know how to respond. I explained to her that they had kept changing prescriptions, as he was not responding to any medication that was prescribed. It was then she burst out, explaining that all that her son got were prescriptions and not medicines. She told me that the Government hospital had no medicines. She could not afford to buy the medicines and her son had not taken any treatment at all.

> I was shell-shocked. It was not 'Idiopathic Hypertension' that had killed her only source of emotional and economic support. It was 'lack of treatment' born of poverty. It was then I realized that all the while, the entire medical team had been discussing his non-responsive condition over the last two months, without actually understanding the root cause. I felt completely lost and hopeless. What kind of medicine was I being trained to practice,

if I could not understand the 'social' and 'economic' dimension of disease and its treatment?

This incident changed my life completely. It was also my first attempt at charity. I collected money from my friends and other 'poor' patients in the ward and helped transport her son's body to her native village.

Further, in the next few days, I decided that I would be my own role model. I would start an organization that would ask these uncomfortable questions and try and find practical and actionable answers. I would start a movement, which would usher in 'ethical, rational and cost-effective' medical care in rural India for people who will be seen as 'people' and not mere sufferers of diseases waiting for treatment.

(http://rbalu.wordpress.com/2009/05/24/6-the-tipping-point/)

The next incident was in November 1984 when Balu was posted as a third year student to Dr. Kaulgud's unit for obstetrics and gynecology. During ward rounds, they were discussing possible approaches to treatment of a patient who was diagnosed with 'anemia of pregnancy'. Balu narrates further,

As the discussion progressed on what kind of iron compound to put this patient on, I burst out saying that we needed to first find out if this patient was taking the medicines after all. For me, this event was sort of déjà vu. I was remembering the hypertensive cook who had died without taking his medicines. Dr. Kaulgud asked me to explain why I felt as I did. I narrated my previous experience to him. I also told him that this patient was the wife of a worker in a textile mill that was 'locked out'. He had taken to alcohol and was a rare visitor to the hospital. With the food that was given to her, she was also feeding her two children. All the prescriptions that were being dished out to her remained just slips of paper. Dr. Kaulgud verified these facts with the patient. He was taken aback on realizing that this was not just anemia that was failing to respond to treatment, it was simple untreated anemia. He told me that his room was full of medicine samples and it was open for me to take and distribute those samples to poor patients.

Here was a man who was a true 'role model' for young medical students like me. He allowed me to see his human side. This incident left a deep impression on me. (http://rbalu.wordpress. com/2009/05/31/8-the-final-push/)

These incidents reflected the real triggers that set off Balu certainty about what he wanted to do with his life to serve society.

Action on the ground: Balu registered Swami Vivekananda Youth Mission (SVYM) at Mysore with the help of his family friend and mentor. On knowing this, Balu's father advised him to study further and gain more experience before experimenting with social work. Balu was firm and his parents finally gave him their blessings to go ahead.

Balu hardly had any money when he landed up in N Begur of Mysore district, in the Western Ghats. A number of good-hearted souls helped him to move. A swamiji of the Ramakrishna Order had given him a cow. A cowshed was constructed to protect it from wild animals.

There were frequent occasions while building a hospital in 1989 at Kenchanahalli they found difficulty in paying wages to the workers. A number of incidents and interfaces with good-hearted people kept the project moving.

In the initial years, Balu's biggest problem was acceptability as a doctor by the tribals. One of the early interfaces was when a pregnant woman delivered a baby in a hamlet of three houses. He wanted to help her achieve safe childbirth. However, this did not happen, as the baby arrived safely before the predicted time. He wanted to see the baby on the following day, but the lady refused entry to him as she was barely dressed and there was no alternate clothing. Balu was moved by this level of abject poverty. It helped him gain strength to stay on and pursue his mission.

Another incident that emphasized the "need to focus" was the response a group of women gave to one of his initiatives. During the initial period, Balu saw a group of about 15 women chatting. He approached them to explain the services he was in a position to provide. As he reached them, they started walking down the hill to a stream to get to the source water. They told him that they may take four to six hours to return and he did not have to wait. He thought that it would be a good step to approach the local administration to get a water tap installed there so that these women need not walk for so long, carrying vessels of water. When he met them after six months, one of the women told him that he had invaded their privacy for four to six hours, as they used this time to share their personal feelings and resolve some of their mutual problems. Balu was shocked that he had never understood their reality; it dawned on him that unsolicited help was not really helping them. This made him to learn to focus his actions on meeting genuine beneficiary needs.

A third incident that helped him gain more acceptability as a doctor was when a snake bit one of the villagers. Balu feels that his efforts to tend to that villager were nothing extraordinary, as the snake was probably of the non-poisonous variety. However, the villagers' attitude towards him changed. They started accepting him as a doctor. It may be useful to note here that during his medical studies, Balu had always questioned the need to seek the "doctor" title. His mentor and Spiritual guru/guide was the person who convinced him to accept an appropriate designation after having come that far.

Family support: Balu stated that his father asked him initially whether his drive to serve society was going to be a passing fantasy or a firm lifetime commitment. When Balu mentioned that it was a lifetime commitment, his father had a balanced reaction. Balu mentions, "To be fair to him and my mother, they never once dissuaded me from doing what I liked. This was indeed great encouragement, coming from a typical middle class family, which always aspired to send their children abroad in search of greener pastures. My sister and brother were equally supportive and have always stood by me. My wife and son are also supportive of my mission and appreciate the time I spend. In fact, they are with me in my work." A number of friends and well-wishers joined him as he progressed.

Conclusion: Dr.Balu, the messiah, is living the belief that *"service to mankind is one way to realize God!"*. He has now transformed SVYM into a multiple-activity development organization undertaking diverse activities. There is a 90-bed hospital at the original site. The hospital provides a number of extended services, including palliative care. There are more than 600 people now working for the movement. SVYM has moved into a number of activities like education in tribal areas by running a school, academics in development education at Mysore, training and research, Indian studies, community development and so on. These efforts have received major recognition across the state and even in other states in India, and a number of policy and advocacy support measures are being provided. Balu travels across the globe talking on issues like development leadership. He passionately talks about how failure to act on the elimination of poverty would be the most serious social crime. He believes that social transformation can happen only if employment generation takes place. He advocates that the three levels of intervention through service—physical, intellectual and spiritual—are critical for human development in any country. Physical service happens in many ways, such as feeding poor people and providing healthcare services. Intellectual service includes services such as providing education and disseminating wisdom and knowledge on matters relating to the rights and responsibilities of a citizen. Spiritual service is the highest level of service, enabling one to look for, find and use internal strengths to solve the problems of the society.

Balu has done it. He was ridiculed, opposed and later accepted. He had the "purity" of thought and action, "patience" in waiting for the right opportunities to melt down challenges and deep "perseverance" even at adverse times. India needs more people like Balu to realize the country's full potential and substantially improve the human development indices!

Footnote:

1. This incredible champion has volumes of content published in his blog. There are different publications on his phenomenal work and personality, going back over the last three decades. With his permission, some of his writings and discussions are captured. The author finds it difficult to give a comprehensive picture of him in this work. However, it is all the more difficult to be not profiling him! The author requests the readers to go to his blog (http://rbalu. wordpress.com/) to learn more about him and his experiences. One may write to him at drrbalu@gmail.com

CHAPTER 19

Death equals all and deserves dignity: Rev.Fr. Thomas Rathappillil, Founder Director, St Joseph's Hospice

Introduction: "Life is precious and beautiful things happen when one distances oneself from negative things" is a quote you might have heard. However, not many of us are lucky enough to live life accordingly. There are many people whose near and dear stopped caring and left them to their fate as they approach life's ultimate departure. These victims do not have a choice. The ordeal of going through both life and death is tough for destitute. However, many of us as fellow humans fail to recognize the pains that they undergo in this process. For some of them, death comes soon; for others, it takes weeks, months and why, even years at times!

Fr. Thomas is a man who shares abundant love and compassion for dying destitute in Tamil Nadu by running a couple of hospice centers.

We will discuss here the trigger, challenges and opportunities faced by Fr. Thomas in extending this service.

Early days:

Born to a Catholic family of nine children, Fr. Thomas Rathappillil lived in Kochi with his family until he was 12 years old. He then moved to Trichy and joined Montfort Brothers of St. Gabriel, a religious society of men established in the year 1716 in France. This society draws inspiration and drive from the vision and audacity of St. Louis Marie de Montfort and Gabriel Dehseyes. It has been working on the task of transforming society through education and empowerment of men, women, youth and children for over two centuries. Its services include health care; primary, secondary and collegiate education; and education of differently abled persons in almost 34 countries of the world. The Brothers go beyond religion, language, caste and other man-made boundaries and serve all people of God, enabling them to live as good persons. Fr. Thomas had his education in Loyola College, Chennai, where he completed his Master in English Literature degree. He then taught for 23 years in different institutions run by the Montfort Brothers. He went to France for higher studies and stayed there for two years, during which time he also learnt French.

Fr. Thomas served in Zaire, a French colony that reverted to its original name, Congo, in 1997. Fr. Thomas learnt Lingala, a language widely spoken in Congo. He was serving the people with dedication; however, challenges came up after the outbreak of communal violence and there was a real threat to his life.

Fr. Thomas moved to Rome and served there for some time. During his time in Europe, he observed how poor homeless people benefitted from "soup kitchens". A soup kitchen offers food free or at below market prices for those who are hungry and cannot afford much or even anything at all. Many of the European countries had social welfare schemes that offered financial support to soup kitchens, enabling the poor to eat in them. The concept became popular and many voluntary societies and religious organizations helped in establishing more of these kitchens.

These organizations had a strong impact on Fr. Thomas. He felt that the poor were receiving assistance that helped them maintain their dignity.

Fr. Thomas moved on to serve as a parish priest at Headingley, Leeds, United Kingdom. He was there for six years.

Trigger: During his service in a church in Leeds, Fr. Thomas suffered a severe heart attack. He underwent a quadruple bypass surgery. The severe cold of England's weather did not help him in matters of health. Doctors advised him that he might live for another decade, but it would be a good idea to return to India where the climate could be more favorable to him. Fr. Thomas took permission from his Bishop and decided to move to Dindigal, near Madurai, to serve in the region.

He joined hands with the famous Aravind Eye Hospitals to work on the "prevention of blindness among rural poor" project. Fr. Thomas employed about 25 people. He traveled to the most remote of villages and arranged for medical attention for people with eye ailments. At one stage, he was instrumental in arranging 400 eye operations in a month. Fr. Thomas credits this achievement to the success of Aravind Eye Hospital in adopting appropriate technology and enabling outreach service in which he and his team could participate. This project became popular, and once government support started pouring in, he decided to focus on other activities.

It was about a decade ago that an incident touched him deeply and set him into introspection. Fr. Thomas and his friend Myrtle Watkins, an English woman who was more like his mother and mentor, were coming out of a restaurant after a meal. To quote Fr. Thomas, "We were shocked to find a man, an apology of a human being, with an arm and leg missing. He was battered, with worms coming out of his body. He was scavenging for scrap from a huge broken plastic bin, battling with stray cows, street dogs and filthy pigs. The sight was terribly disturbing." [1]

He recalled his experience watching people who lived in tents and under bridges in developed nations with cold climates. These people could battle life out with the financial support of government support and because they had "soup kitchens" to go to. All of these people had an identity and a social security cover to protect them. Unfortunately, it will take time in India for such social security cover to be available to all, including destitute. Until such a time, these deprived souls will continue to suffer unaided!

Watkins, who had known Fr. Thomas since he was 27 years old, decided to support his idea of starting a hospice. She wrote out a check for forty thousand pounds. It took five years from that point in time to launch the hospice.

Opportunities and challenges: The hospice is located in the Sirumalai Hills in Dindigul District. It is an amazing environment with a refreshing breeze and strong natural light. The area is full of natural vegetation, which is ideally suited for relaxing and soothing sick patients.

Fr. Thomas says, "The first patient I found was lying outside the Government Hospital, Madurai. His brain was affected by septicemia, sores covered his body and gangrene had eaten off his forearm. He lived for only two days, but we cleaned him, fed him well and showered him with all love and respect."

Most of the times, his patients are far from normal human conditions. Often, they are people who were ignored or disowned by their families because of poverty. Hospitals they were admitted to were not in a position to carry their treatment forward, as they did not respond. Though the hospitals did their best to maintain support, physical frailties were a limiting factor.

It is not death itself, but the passage of time being terminally ill and waiting for death—that could be days, weeks or even months long—that is so cruel to these patients.

Fr. Thomas continuously gets calls and alerts from hospitals and other well-wishers about destitute folk who need attention. He picks them up in an ambulance and brings them to his hospice. He generally takes patients who are not affected by infectious diseases, as he has inmates who are already sick and susceptible. In case he comes across such patients, he refers them to other centers that are equipped to handle them.

Challenges include finding and training appropriate staff to run the center. It may be noted that Fr. Thomas has identified and appointed dedicated staff who support him in all his endeavors. To quote him, "earlier, we used to go around looking for diseased and abandoned people on the streets and bring them in. Now, shopkeepers, autowallahs, bus-drivers and passers-by inform us and we rush to the spot. Once they are brought to the hospice, their wounds are bandaged, they are given the appropriate medication and they are washed thoroughly, shaved, dressed afresh and fed a wholesome meal. Their ragged clothes are burnt. Every individual's specific needs are taken care of. Some cannot see, others cannot walk, and a few are too feeble to rise from their beds. We nurse the sick with all love and devotion. We use wheelchairs and Zimmer frames to take the infirm out to the lawns. Our aim is to restore their self-respect in their final days."

He does not have a long roster of staff. He has trained nursing staff who multitask. He introduced the author to one of his staff, who functions like professional managers in carrying out her responsibilities for managing the hospice accounts, running the administration and providing other guidance needed for smooth functioning. Over and above, she also takes care of the children there. Though the hospice is not chartered to administer to children, there are a few inmates with families, and their children need to be taken care of. Another staff member he introduced is a trained nurse. She also works as a caretaker and further, is capable of driving the ambulance in emergencies. She has the required license to do so. Such is the dedication of the staff Fr. Thomas employs.

Fr. Thomas is proud to point out that he works along with all of them as just another staff member. There is no hierarchy of power. In fact, he is also responsible for delivering tasks and accounts to the administration in charge. The system is so well maintained that whenever he travels on a mission, his staff members take up his responsibilities without a glitch.

There is much opportunity for improvement, but Fr. Thomas needs generous support from volunteers to set about it. There are about 325 inmates at the Dindigal hospice and more than 120 inmates in Uthiramerur, Chengalpet district. All of them are served meals three times a day, besides a mid-day snack. Since Fr. Thomas uses traditional cooking methods, he could use help in setting up a modern, improvised kitchen. Though he is aware of this need, limitations in his current staffing situation hinder adoption of new technologies.

He himself is highly oriented towards adoption of modern technology. He has erected a concrete burial system where dead bodies are inserted in a vault. The vault system has multiple slots, and bodies are inserted in sequence. Each filled slot is closed and cemented airtight. This system is completely environment friendly. There is no impact on the earth or on water in the environment. After some years, when the bodies have decayed, the bones are extracted and burnt. He has seen this system gaining popularity elsewhere in India and around the world. It is important to understand this, as he handles at least six deaths a week in Dindigal and about four deaths a week in Chengalpet.

It is mindboggling to see how he and his staff handle the emotional needs of the inmates under all circumstances. Most of them are pathetic and weak, and some are mentally unstable. They are showered with love. The challenge to the staff is humongous, to say the least. About 35% of the inmates have no control over their urinary and bowel movements. They keep the staff busy cleaning up the place; over and above these physical issues, the staff must attend to the inmates' emotional demands as well.

The other challenge we observed lies in satisfying financial needs. It requires a lot of money to run centers of this size. Until about two years ago, Fr. Thomas used to get donations from Europe. With the economic slowdown, the hospices' funds position is strained. He mentioned the fact that now a number of Indians are contributing to his operations, which are agnostic in terms of religion. Funding is a key challenge in keeping the hospices running.

One other aspect worth noting is that some of the inmates recover and live longer than initially expected. They do not have any relatives or friends to fall back on, and thus, cannot rejoin the mainstream. They do not have official or social identification. They stay on at the center, rendering support activities. There are some moving instances, like the case of Santhanam, a meat shop owner, who ran into his wife Radha again after they were separated by ill luck. Both had developed physical and mental challenges and had problems in identifying each other, though Santhanam, in spite of being blind, identified his wife!

This author experienced great courtesy at the hospice. After they done with the tour, an attendant insisted that they must dine there. What was touching was her humility when she expressed the pleasure she would derive if they ate there.

Fr. Thomas bought the land for building the Dindigal hospice. The land on which the Chengalpat hospice is situated was a donation from a good-hearted person. He intends to build one more hospice near Tambaram, as there are many more patients in Chennai.

Learning: When asked about the challenges faced in ensuring professionalization at the hospices, Fr. Thomas is humble. He says he thinks and acts for the moment. For him, service is of paramount importance. He mentions that he leaves the future in the hands of God. He has another two Jesuit priests as his trustees, both past 80 years of age. The cardiac intervention Fr. Thomas went through was not going to stop him from his good work. When this author asked about the future plans for a resident two-year-old boy, Jobin, Fr. Thomas stated that Jobin is a part of their family, and has been adopted by one of his staff members. He wonders if it is God's design that one day in the future, Jobin may take over the management of these hospices. The positive aggression and optimism he shows are what drive the spirit of these places.

Conclusion: Fr. Thomas mentioned that when we look at death, life becomes meaningless. He has subdued death by ensuring that destitute who are kissing death are able to do so with peace and dignity. He is philosophical when he says that death equates all souls, whether rich or poor, men, women or child, healthy or diseased. It is important to facilitate people to take their final rest in peace. According to him, we cannot know the destiny of a soul after it departs. What we can do is ensure that it departs in peace. Noble is the thinking of Fr. Thomas, noble is the service rendered by him and his staff, and noble is his commitment and kindness towards neglected people. This world would be a far better place for the aged, the infirm and the neglected to live in if only there were more benefactors like Fr. Thomas around us!

Reference:

1. Touching lives, celebrating love, http://www.thehindu.com/features/metroplus/society/touching-lives-celebrating-love/article840768.ece

CHAPTER 20

Restoring dignity among destitute: Narayanan Krishnan, Founder, Akshaya Trust

Introduction: Well may you wonder what else a man could do after completing his education and starting a career as a chef in a five star hotel! You would expect him to pursue the advancement of his career. You would expect him to be madly excited about an opportunity to work in Switzerland with a leading international chain of hotels, especially if he was born to an affluent family and was groomed with lots of ambition. Then, when you get to know the reality, you may call it the hand of god or a twist of fortune or fate, when such a person gets recognition as a real life hero by CNN Heroes—Everyday People Changing the World. The person we are about to discuss was among 10 heroes chosen by CNN in 2010. He is Narayanan Krishnan from Madurai—a highly energetic man with a deep sense of commitment and empathy for destitute! He works on the salvation of the poor from a state of despair by providing relief and peace.

Early days: Krishnan is from an affluent family. He had a happy childhood. His father K. Narayanan is a retired insurance agent and his mother, Lakshmi, is an administrative officer with a government-owned insurance company. His parents instilled a strong sense of responsibility and discipline in him, right from his early childhood. By observing his mother, Krishnan understood, even in his childhood, the importance of staying engaged with meaningful work. He learned never to think of a job as just a mere source of income. He learned to do everything with a deep sense of love and pride. He approached his studies also with the same attitude, and thus, he thoroughly enjoyed them.

Somewhere along the line in his early growth stage, he realized that he had great interest in becoming a hotel management professional, especially in the area of food and beverages. He was excited about becoming a chef. Actually, this was not a common choice for someone with his family background and even more so, for someone coming from his kind of conservative society.

However, his parents encouraged him to pursue whatever interests excited him. He has a charming and pleasant personality. He is energetic and has resolved to progress with passion with his choices. Even in his childhood, his parents thought, rightfully, that he was capable of realizing his dreams. Krishnan is a loving family-oriented person and has a sister, Shweta Narayanan. From his earliest days, Krishnan was deeply caring about his family and kept all of them bound together with cheer, humor and love.

Krishnan says about himself:

> I received a very good education from a reputed school in Madurai, and did my bachelors' course in hotel management from Madurai Kamaraj University. After that, I had the opportunity of working with a group of five-star hotels in Bangalore from where I was also supposed to go to Europe to work s a chef.

All of a sudden, an impulse triggered him to move to working in the social sector. We now discuss what sent him down the social service path.

Defining moment for change: Almost invariably, you will find that every person involved with the social sector was triggered to do so by some factor or other. This gave them a strong urge to dedicate themselves to something unique, or something demanding deep conviction and dedication to carry out. Krishnan also experienced such a defining moment; it made him dedicate himself to changing the world around him to a better place for people to whom it mattered.

Krishnan narrates this incident:

> I did not have any idea about this path or any plans to choose this journey by setting up an organization. It all happened because of an incident that touched my heart, and after that, my inner voice insisted that I enter the gateway of giving.

> In June 2002, while travelling on a busy road in Madurai, I saw an old man eating his own human waste out of hunger. I was completely shaken and oblivious to my surroundings. I jumped out of my vehicle and, went to the old man. I realized he was driven by acute hunger and was not in a proper shape of mind. Immediately I bought a few idlis (steam-cooked pudding) and gave them to him. As the old man gobbled the food given to him at a speed I had not experienced before, he held my hands, giving me very real sensation that he was transmitting love and energy, something I had never felt before. That inner happiness and fulfillment changed my life forever. This deeply etched unique experience is vivid even now.

As anyone would look at it, this was an experience that would have agonized any fellow human. A typical Good Samaritan response in similar circumstances is to give some money or buy some food just for that one time, maybe accompanied by a few words of love. That was what Krishnan did, but with him, it did not stop there. This event triggered a decision to forgo his career opportunity abroad. He chose to remain, to listen to his heart and nourish neglected humans out in the streets. The difference in Krishnan was that where passion should have helped him to earn wealth, he turned to using his wealth to feed destitute! This was an astonishing, truly heroic transformation in the life of a man who was then in his twenties!

Determined moves: For the first few months, Krishnan dug into his savings and bought food to distribute to the helpless poor. He traveled in his car along the roads of Madurai district, distributing food. He narrates this experience as follows:

> I started off as a one-man army in the year 2002 with the money I had saved. Initially, I bought food from roadside shops and distributed it. From January 2003, for reasons of economy and hygiene, I started cooking the food by myself at the back of my house and distributed it in the morning, at noon and in the evening.
>
> At the beginning, I was feeding less than 20 people a day. I did everything by myself, from purchasing, cutting vegetables, cooking, packing and even delivering.
>
> Once the number of people I was serving increased to 50, a young boy named Mani joined me to help me cope with all of them without compromising on the quality of the food. As the numbers increased, I employed more people.

One must consider the transformational challenges Krishnan underwent. From acting on an emotional reaction to looking at a painful event to making it a habit to feed the destitute and homeless of Madurai, and then to quitting his career to act on this passion, he was required to cross a number of hurdles.

Let us understand how his friends, relatives and parents felt as he launched his social work as a fulltime effort. He fed more than 50 people going around in a car on certain routes to cater to the poorest of the poor, people who were languishing on the pavements of village roads or living in abandoned large pipes or just anywhere they happened to be. These people did not have access to facilities for a proper wash and other basic hygiene. They see god on being served food and live for the moment.

Krishnan did not stop at giving food. He started sponsoring haircuts and shaves. He got his beneficiaries to wash, and made them feel fresh. These are not easy things to do, and they cannot be done every day. Even when one does these things selectively, it is difficult to imagine sustaining the drive required to continue with such a service. How many of us allow ourselves to even get close to such humans, let alone render them such a service? It requires tremendous drive, fearlessness and ability to serve selflessly. One needs to be fearless because one should not worry about what others think, or about likely infections that may occur when handling homeless humans. Imagine what Krishnan must have been thinking when doing it for the first time. From just buying food for destitutes to offering them food and hygiene—it is nothing like shop floor add-on service. You read about such services more in fantasies and works of fiction! Krishnan not only made it a reality but also made it a routine, a habit. Krishnan's challenge was in committing himself full time and systematizing his work.

Surmounting the challenges:

Over the first few months, there was no support for Krishnan. In fact, there was strong opposition from close friends and relatives. To quote Krishnan,

> My act was considered abnormal and out of alignment. My family was opposed to my decision. Coming from the upper echelon of society, this was not a typical career path and my parents, too, like any other parents, had big dreams for me. Their hopes and dreams were crushed by my decision. I decided to take my mother on my service rounds one day and when she saw the pain, the hunger, and when a few of those I served fell at her feet and thanked her for my help, she realized that what I

was involved in was something amazing. She promised to feed me while I took care of the helpless.

Krishnan had to listen to his heart and stay with his mission. He had to balance his commitment towards his family, their values and dreams with his passion to pursue his philanthropy. Krishnan thought, rightly, that his mother, who had always inspired him with her commitment to value, was the right person to start with. He had decided that to win support, it was important to make doubters realize the truth of the experience in person. Krishnan was convinced that he could transmit the energy and drive he felt to his mother. He believed that he would receive her blessings and endorsement after she had firsthand experience. This belief turned out to be true. After taking his mother, he then took his father through the same experience. He says, "To this day, my parents stand by me in all my decisions. My father often runs errands for Akshaya". Krishnan's grooming and self-confidence helped him to negotiate the first set off barricades.

Slowly, Krishnan's friends also started to understand his mission and encouraged him. After a while, Krishnan never had time for any of his stakeholders. Once he started cooking and delivering food himself, he became very busy. His typical day would start at 4.00 a.m., when he went out to buy vegetables. He then started preparing for cooking by cutting vegetables and organizing everything necessary for preparation of the meals. He would do everything himself, as he had passion for cooking. Then Krishnan packed the food in small single servings to hand out as he drove to his various delivery points. He used to drive 60-70 km every day to finish handing over the food packets to his beneficiaries. It was not an easy job, when he had to do it without consideration of monetary benefits.

As he started serving more people, the size of his kitchen in the backyard of his home became inadequate. He had to rent a suitable place and hire people to help him. Such a level required management skills in organizing resources like material, men and money. He invested whatever he could, and received generous support from his parents. Slowly, his friends also started chipping in. He never asked money from anyone.

To quote Krishnan on resource constraints,

> Initially when I was alone, I did not have any blueprints or plans. I just pushed myself to give joy and happiness to the people who needed care.

> According to me, no research is required to do good to the society. It is just a matter of answering your inner voice to help the needy to the best possible extent of an individual— sometimes research will not serve the purpose and will become a never-ending subject.

> No good cause will ever stop of want of any resources. If a good cause stops for want of any resources, the cause is not good enough, and has to be improved.

This statement of Krishnan shows his deep conviction about his role in making life meaningful for others. One need not think that benevolence involves just soft corners. It requires hard, practical attitudes to be different in thinking, acting and visualizing the end result. This is so different from living just for the self and a small group around.

Scaling up:

During this process, Krishnan formed an organization, the Akshaya Trust. Krishnan and Akshaya have prepared and delivered three meals a day every day of the year for ten years. As of 2013, they have delivered over 1,900,000 meals whether rain was pouring down or the sun was blazing.

Akshaya is now feeding approximately 450 people a day. Over time, Krishnan has redesigned his approach to enable better use of resources that are under his command. Instead of cooking and delivering food in vans like in the case of milk and water distribution, he envisaged the possibility that he could bring all beneficiaries under one roof and thus, serve them better. It also gave them an opportunity to socialize and feel like they were part of a community.

Working on this thought, Krishnan conceived of the idea of building the Akshaya Home for destitutes. The Akshaya Home will be a shelter for the homeless, a haven for the sick and a place to provide additional continuous care for those in need. The site preparation started in 2009 and building construction started in 2010. As of 2013, it houses about 450 people. It required a lot of governance, fund raising capability, discipline in project management and an ability to convert vision and mission into strategy. Krishnan provides such strategic leadership.

Cooking meals for 450 people would be a major task for a well-staffed restaurant with the best of equipment. For Krishnan and the volunteers at Akshaya Trust, it is a routine done three times a day with minimal staff, very basic equipment and in less than an hour for each meal (http://www.akshayatrust.org/feeding.php). If one happens to visit this home, which is about 20 km away in the outskirts of Madurai, one would be surprised to see the cleanliness and hygiene, and the involvement of destitute folks along with staff in preparation of the food.

In fact, all occupants ensure that they keep the place neat and clean. Their mindset is calm and their spirits are motivated and high. They practice yoga, walk around, play, talk and pray as a community. It looks simple but is very challenging for the staff. When a new person is picked up to join the home from the streets, he or she is often not in the right mental frame, and may be suffering from fragile health. Not all residents share a common language. They are housed in a dormitory. There is a health centre with medical facilities, and some of them are admitted there at various times. There is a lab inside for routine investigations and records are maintained scrupulously to comply with statutory requirements.

During most of the day, Krishnan is on the spot, walking around and living along with the residents, cheering them up and ensuring that the mission stays successful. His challenge now is staffing the activity. He has about 40 employees in the trust, and it is a challenge to keep staff size appropriate for increasing resident size. He mentors these people and helps them understand how to be compassionate with the people in the home. Such leadership is demanding, and he balances his time and resources to ensure optimum achievement of the overall objectives of his mission. He has committed trustees and staff who support his endeavors.

Akshaya Trust employees go on a round in an ambulance three times a week and rescue people who are on the streets. Usually, they come across a few such people on every trip. Out of the more than 700 people who have been picked up, more than a 100 have been reunited with their families, after receiving care and nourishment from Akshaya. About 50 of them left this world, and final respects were paid at the home. The government has given Akshaya Home permission to pick people up off the streets, provided everything is reported. There are statutory formalities in place that must be complied with. On arrival, every person gets lots of love and affection, and an essential part of the reception is to get him or her clean and hygienic. Food and shelter follow. Krishnan personally gets involved in most cases. This author observed all of this during an unannounced visit to the place—evidence of the abundance of love and peace with which new entrants are received.

Family support: As mentioned earlier, Krishnan's parents and sister give immense support. It took a while to win their support, but once they were convinced, they were firmly committed. Krishnan was married in January 2011 to Harini, and has since been blessed with a girl baby, Sara. His wife supports him by encouraging him to pursue his dream, even though he hardly gets time for home. He is not in a regular 40-hour-per-week job. He is engaged 24 X 7 with the Akshaya Home and the people there. His celebrations and joys are first at the Akshaya Home. His family members are accustomed to this situation, and enjoy whatever time they get with him. For a social entrepreneur, family time becomes the most important aspect of balancing personal life with mission.

Conclusion: Krishnan's deeds are heroic. He has charm, energy, leadership traits and the ability to fight against the isolation of people neglected by the society in a small part of India. His mission is commendable, and worthy of replication elsewhere. Additionally, Krishnan has the daunting challenge of sustaining his success in ensuring that there are no homeless people in Madurai district. We all know that the government machinery works for such people. However, the governmental set up has its own limitations, considering bureaucratic demands and other pressures. I hope this mission of Krishnan will continue to succeed and grow. The world needs more Krishnans to achieve social justice and universal humanity.

CHAPTER 21

Serving to bring hope, comfort and love: Deepa Muthaiya, Founder, Dean Foundation

A **woman of substance**: It has been said that very strong bonds have been forged between granddaughters and grandmothers—proving to be powerful and meaningful for many years.

Such was the relationship Deepa shared with her grandma—Dr. Adaline Micah. Her holidays spent in Tirupati where her grandma practiced, were something she looked forward to, with excitement, every year. More than anything else, memories of Dr. Micah, in her crisp cotton saree, tending to the patients and mixing magic potions in glass bottles remains etched in her memory. People stood in long queues to see her. She recalls frantic knocks in the dead of the night, summoning her grandma to attend to a medical emergency in someone's house. After a hard night, she was back as fresh as a daisy in her clinic the next morning. Her grandma was a woman of substance! Deepa loved and admired her deeply.

"Where are such doctors, these days?" Deepa wondered. "Can a poor family expect a doctor to come to their little shack, that too in the dead of the night, at this point in time? And that too in metropolitan cities like in Chennai?"

Her formative years: During the holidays, apart from watching her grandma with adoring eyes, she spent time reading books. She was a voracious reader and devoured books so fast that friends and family had a tough time keeping the books flowing! She developed her love of reading from her father, J.K. Pavithran, who encouraged her to be independent and versatile. He lost no opportunity in giving her the best. Her mother, Sheila, was a strict disciplinarian. Both stressed the importance of education and high academic excellence. Mediocre performance was looked down upon.

Deepa was born in Renigunta, Andhra Pradesh, and she grew up in Nilgiris. She moved with her parents to Chennai, completed her Pre-University Course in SIET Women's College and soon joined Ethiraj College for Women. She joined Karate, the NCC, learnt flying and threw herself into college life with enthusiasm. She valued friendships. She excelled in writing poems and stories, and won a few awards. At the end of the first year in college, she got married and soon after, became a mother of a son. With a break of a year, she continued with her education. After her second son was born, she went on to do her masters in English literature and thereafter another in journalism and communication. Every day, she cooked for the family, dropped her children in school and went to college, picking them on her way back, and cooked again. Life was tough, but she persisted against all odds to complete her Master of Philosophy as a regular student. She says she owes her education to her husband, her teachers and her friends, without whom she could not have succeeded to finish her courses.

Her early life revealed her grit and determination to complete any task she undertook, successfully. Her resilience in the face of all odds is amply demonstrated in what DEAN Foundation has become today. She does not believe in short cuts or cutting corners but goes into the details of every task, much to the dismay of her staff. Her skill in multitasking helped her juggle her roles as a mother, wife and student. Yet she made time to reach out to help others, to visit friends in hospital, take food, listen to people's woes, and help them network with those who could help.

While working in a Paging company, she rescued a customer who was an alcoholic and got him rehabilitated. Another customer was on the verge of committing suicide. She reached out to the man and found that his marriage plans had been abandoned by the bride's family, because his mother had suddenly expired. He had by then grown to love the lady who he thought would be his wife! Deepa made him see reason and encouraged him every day with messages of inspiring quotes on his Pager. She had never met this man, but one day, many years later, he walked into DEAN Foundation with sweets to say that he was a father of a baby boy!

Her inspiration: While nursing a relative in hospital, she came across a book called the *Tibetan Book of the Living and Dying*, by Sogyal Rinpoche. The book changed her destiny and introduced her into the new medical specialty called Palliative Medicine. Palliative medicine has been promoted by the World Health Organization (WHO) as a comprehensive, multidisciplinary manner of care offered by a team of doctors, nurses, social workers, volunteers and members of religious orders. The accent is on total control of pain and alleviation of social, psychological and spiritual problems.

In the foreword to *Tibetan Book of the Living and Dying*, His Holiness the Dalai Lama writes, "Naturally, most of us would like to die a peaceful death, but it is also clear that we cannot hope to die peacefully if our lives have been full of violence, or if our minds have mostly been agitated by emotions like anger, attachment, or fear. So if we wish to die well, we must learn how to live well: hoping for a peaceful death, we must cultivate peace in our mind, and in our way of life."

He continued, ". . . No less significant than preparing for our own death, is helping others to die well. As a newborn baby each of us was helpless and, without the care and kindness we received then, we would not have survived. Because the those who are dying also unable to help themselves, we should relieve them of discomfort and anxiety, and assist them, as far as we can, to die with composure."

Rinpoche writes in his foreword to the second edition, "my original hope for this book was that it would help inspire a quiet revolution in the whole way we look at death and care for the dying, and so the whole way we look at life and care for the living . . . What would be the effect of seeking to make love and compassion the measure of our every action, and of understanding, to any degree, the inmost nature of the mind that underlies our entire existence?"

Talking about Deepa, Rinpoche also goes on to mention how a lady in Madras, started a Hospice after reading the book.

Deeply moved and touched by the book, she wanted to care for the dying and did not know where to begin. A relative's chance mention of the field of palliative medicine being a new specialty in UK, set her on a path—a "road less travelled."

She remembered her grandmother's work and brooded over, how in today's world a poor family living in a hut, a Plastic tent or on the pavement, could get a Doctor to visit their humble "home?"

Deepa relating this wondered whether it would be possible, in these fast-paced times, for a common man or for that matter anyone to get a doctor to visit someone at home. But how would terminally, progressive ill patients manage? She thought of providing hospice and palliative care services to those who desperately needed it, in the place they called "home!"

Hospice and palliative care: Hospice care is a philosophy of care practised using the guiding principles of palliative medicine. Hospice and palliative care services are required throughout the course of a serious illness, regardless of access to disease-modifying treatment. It covers a variety of responses including providing physical, psychological, social, legal and spiritual support, supporting both people and their carers throughout the course of the illness.

Palliative care is a cross-cutting issue that is a vital component of an effective and functioning health system, ensuring end-of-life quality, ensuring productivity of people living with life limiting conditions and their families. Hospice services are characterized by a team-oriented approach that includes expert pain and symptom management, along with emotional and spiritual support tailored to the patient's wishes. The most common misunderstanding about hospice is the belief that a hospice is a "place." In fact, most patients receive hospice care in their own home, although it can also be provided in other facilities as well.

Deepa's desired to provide medical care for people with advanced cancer, end-stage diabetes, chronically ill and frail elderly people, HIV-related illness, or other diseases so that they regain some control over their lives and to improve and stabilize distressing symptoms.

Thus by taking a medical team led by a doctor, to patients' homes, no matter where they lived, Deepa was emulating what her grandma used to do, all those years ago.

First steps: The word DEAN is an acronym for Dignify and Empower the Ailing and the Needy. The trust was conceived to be an oasis for those who were in need of solace. It was meant to be a place offering nonjudgmental, unconditional love and understanding—provided free of charge—to all irrespective of their economic or religious background. Lofty ideals needing untiring focus and commitment!

DEAN Foundation went through severe birthing pangs. Deepa first shared dreams with two family friends, Rotarian and Past District Governor, Mr. K.V. Srinivasan, UNIPRO and Mr. K. Aravindan, Engineering Services Manager, Chennai Container Terminal. Both agreed with her vision of caring for those with life-threatening illness and the dying. They came together to register the trust on March 1998 and named it "DEAN Foundation". Raising funds for the work was tough. Deepa left her job to devote all her working hours to building the trust. After her initial funds were spent, it was Arvindan who offered to help. Her husband and relatives pitched in whenever possible. Donors felt that donating to a cause like hospice was a waste.

Finding a place for rent was difficult. House owners were afraid of patients dying on their premises. Neighbours objected. Advertising for medical staff brought no doctors or nurses. Three doctors came in succession and went. A lot of money was wasted in their travel and training. Only the fourth doctor stayed. Work began in a two-roomed accommodation in Kilpauk, with no furniture. Since DEAN was a stand-alone NGO, not attached to any hospital, Deepa had to meet doctors personally to convince them to refer patients.

Today patients bring in more patients!

Deepa herself went to London, met the pioneer of the Modern Hospice Movement, Dame Cicely Saunders and spent over a week in St. Christopher's Hospice learning about managing a hospice service. She also visited three other hospices in Vienna where she acquired different perspectives of the subject. Unfortunately, Mr. Srinivasan, who had accompanied her to London and travelled onwards to USA, died there after a massive heart attack. Deepa sought support of another senior doctor by name Dr. Biswakumar, an eminent neurophysician who had lost his wife to cancer. Deepa invited him to become a trustee in Mr. K.V. Srinivasan's place.

Like any other organization, she had a great challenge in putting together resources namely money, staff and volunteers. Mr. Aravindan was a phenomenal support. He used to give part of his salary for the functioning of DEAN Foundation. Getting morphine tablets for pain relief was impossible without a license. When she applied for the license to the collector's office, they came for inspection. They did not see rows and rows of beds. The concept of home care was alien to the officials. Deepa took one of the officials on a home care visit. The lady was so touched by what she witnessed, that the license was given immediately. Nothing came easy. Building up DEAN Foundation was one long, roller coaster ride!

Deepa with help of the Senior Citizens's Association of Kipauk invited all the Heads of the State government and brought about a landmark amendment of the Narcotics Act. The Indian Association of Palliative Care and the Pain and Policy Studies Group, Wisconsin, congratulated Deepa's efforts for bring about an amendment in a record time of seven months and thus improving the availability and access to opioid analgesics in the State of Tamil Nadu. DEAN Foundation's role created history in Tamil Nadu.

She was loved by her patients who were reluctant to let her go after each visit. The third patient donated his old Fiat to the trust, because she said, she had to leave as the auto was waiting!

Unfortunately, Mr. Arvindan died a few years back of blood cancer. It was one blow after another. But Deepa was not a person to give up. She doubled her efforts to keep the work of the trust going. She invited Dr. Ravi Sundar George to take Arvindan's place.

Deepa soon realised her limitations in dreaming that no one, even those living in the remotest village, should die in pain and suffering. She realized that the best way of doing this was to join hands with the governmental healthcare system.

She sensitized heads of government in the need for hospice and palliative care services in the governmental healthcare system, at the first meeting on February 2010, convened by the State Health and Family Welfare Department, for the creation of Palliative Care Policy for the State of Tamil Nadu. Though not a doctor herself, she chose to tread the ground that many feared. Under her leadership, DEAN Foundation set up the first Rural Outreach Palliative Project in a Government Primary Health Centre in the District of Kancheepuram, Tamil Nadu, on December 2009. They were the first NGO to be offered space in the Public Health Centre by the Director of Public Health and Preventive Medicine in the state, and it was the first palliative care project in the state government healthcare system.

She further convinced the government to allow her to travel with a medical team throughout Tamil Nadu, and she helped set up designated Palliative Care Units in all the government Teaching College Hospitals, in all the districts, from 10 Dec. 2010. This was a big achievement, never attempted by any state ever before, especially when even a policy was not in place!

As part of the service, the care of terminally ill children resulted in Deepa being conferred the Elizabeth Kubler Ross award in 2003, by the

Children's Hospice International, Virginia, USA. In continuation with this effort evolved the idea of a Paediatric Hospice. This award gave her the much needed confidence to set up the first paediatric palliative care centre in the state, in the heart of a government Children's Hospital, on April 2010. The challenge was staffing the unit, financing the unit and running it under the banner of DEAN Foundation. It was an innovative model.

On May 2013 after evaluating the successful execution of hospice and palliative care services of DEAN Foundation in Kancheepuram district, the government of Tamil Nadu has announced in the State Assembly to set up palliative care centers in all districts in the state. This brought great solace to Deepa who now knew that slowly, relief of pain and suffering to the needy was becoming a reality.

Family support: Her husband, Suresh, is a pillar of support and completely understands her work and has been a supporter by encouraging her to spend time with patients. Her sons who are now living abroad are encouraging Deepa to continue with her commitment to DEAN Foundation, offering encouragement and financial support. Apart from family, there are a number of professionals and friends who have helped her with time and resources. Of course, the challenge lies in making DEAN Foundation sustainable. There are issues in resource mobilization, getting human resource and supportive leadership for strategizing growth.

Conclusion: Deepa has been serving the society in a niche area of health care. The domain is difficult for the best of administrators and medical professionals to venture into! Giving dignity to the dying is easily said than done! Her earnest attempt to improve coverage and access is phenomenal. The need for such a service is continuously increasing. Resource crunch in health care for the seriously ill is fast catching up. Nuclear families lack the support a joint family would have given! Spaces in urban homes come at a premium. With likely increase of terminally and progressively ill patients in absolute numbers, with increase in the elderly population the world needs more centres and people like Deepa!

CHAPTER 22

Love for less cared old age humans: Bhageerathy Ramamoorthy, Founder, Anandam Trust

Introduction: When we are young, we are full of energy and hope. We have the fire and potential to accomplish a lot many things in life. However, we do this best when we are fortunate enough to have had enough opportunities to make a good living. Here we define good living as fulfilment of economic and emotional needs for our immediate families. In Indian society, the family includes not only the nucleus of husband, wife and children, but also elderly parents and other dependents. However, changing phases of the economy, increasing trends toward nuclear families and adoption of westernized culture are taking a toll on family values and structures. Increasingly, elders are left to fend for themselves as emotional bondages erode. Things get worse when the elders fail to sympathise with the aspirations of their children's economic ambitions and of the pressure of the competitive world to measure up in terms of wealth creation and education of children.

While these instances of reality are not yet the accepted way of life here, as in western nations, they are becoming increasingly common. Pressures are extreme for single-child parents whose child has settled abroad. Disconnects happen even in evolved families who are more value driven.

Now imagine the plight of older people who are victims of the changes in Indian culture and family systems. There are old age homes available to citizens who can afford them. However, not many people are that fortunate in the financial sense. Whatever the reasons, there are many single elders and even couples who have neither economic independence nor reliable support from their own progeny or siblings. Where do these people go to live out their remaining lives in comfort and with honour? It is common to see such people suffering without a proper home.

Bhageerathy Ramamoorthy has long been motivated to do some exemplary work in addressing the issue of homeless elders, with the support of a few others. In this chapter, we see how Bhageerathy's services to the deprived elderly, evolved.

Formative Years: Bhageerathy was born in a typical Hindu family with high values for elders. She grew up in a joint family, where her parents served the family elders with respect and care. During her formative years, it was routine to pray and dine with the elders, and listen attentively when they spoke. She assumed that this was the way of life! She understood that the only things elders seek are love and care from their younger ones. For her, elders had nothing but good wishes for their young ones, but did expect the young ones to hear their views.

First shock: Bhageerathy lived her early years in Ambattur, then an outskirt of Chennai. After graduation, she joined a nationalized bank in 1979. She proved to be very popular with the bank's customers. In 1994, there was a change in her orientation towards humans based on a few observations. She saw elderly people lining up in front of the bank at 4 a.m. in the morning to collect a meagre pension of Rs. 500 per month, even though the bank would only open at 9 a.m. There were even worse aspects of the problems faced by these pensioners. All of them had lists of payments to make, for which the budgets sanctioned by their children were not enough. Bhageerathy found the lists pathetic, with items such as payments for coffee, snacks, and small gift. Month after month, Bhageerathy observed that as soon as the elders collected their pensions, someone (mostly from their families) would snatch away the money making some or other claim and leave them in distress. She could only sympathize and wonder about these degradations in family values. How could these elders not feel emotionally let down, when they could not enjoy economic freedom and dignity?

Being persuasive and action driven: Her husband Ramamoorthy is an air conditioning and refrigeration engineer. Hers was a typical middle-class family with high values; however, she was not sure how she could help aged people who were suffering. Desire was strong, but there was uncertainty about how to proceed. She spoke to her friends like Rajkumar (of Thalassaemic Society of Tamil Nadu and Association of Voluntary Blood Donors, a personality profiled in chapter 15 of this book) who was a strong motivator and her colleague at work. On his assurance of support, she mustered courage and spoke to her father of her intention to run an old age home with her income. However, her father advised her to first settle down to family life. Bhageerathy then spoke to her husband, who was encouraging and advised her to pursue her desires and make them a reality. Meanwhile, she was transferred to a different branch, even as her family grew with the birth of their two children.

Relentless efforts bore fruits! She was transferred back to a branch near her home. On seeing her determination, one of her acquaintances offered her home to get the project going. Bhageerathy did not hesitate even for a second. Had she paused to worry over how she would fund and operate a project to provide support to an extended family of elderly people, she probably would never have begun. It called for an impromptu decision to start action, and she rose to the challenge!

Deep desire to give shape: Though she first formed and registered the Anandam Trust in 1995, the action really began in 2003 with three residents. She faced huge challenges in providing food, security and health care for the three residents. She had to manage everything without any corpus or guaranteed financial support. Bhageerathy extended support from her own kitchen. Her family and friends also took turns at feeding the residents. She requested her neighbours to provide watch-and-ward support. She trained residents to send out an alert when they needed help and provided them with a phone. She also made arrangements with a doctor to visit them when called for.

Though all this sounds simple, it was quite complicated in reality. She could not miss a single session of feeding or support giving. Bhageerathy managed everything with the extended support of her friends, a few of whom became trustees of her organization.

She slowly increased the size of her operations by leasing more houses in the same area and by increasing the number of residents to 20 over a period of 18 months. Even at that stage, all of the residents were provided food from her's and her friends' kitchen. Each person would make one food item and add it to the pool for the residents' meals. Bhageerathy had such charisma that she was successful in weaving together a network of volunteers who helped with her cause.

Strong will to scale up: You may have noted that she named her trust "Anandam", which means happiness. It caters to people who have no one else to fall back on. Seeing her maintain her noble service even in the face of paucity of funds, more residents wanted to move into Anandam for its excellence in showering residents with love and affection. Bhageerathy had to keep arranging larger space to enable the trust to house more residents.

She developed the routine of devoting one hour in the morning and one hour in the evening to look for suitable plots for the trust's building.

Mr. K. Narayanan, one of the trustees also contributed a lot towards this. It was no easy task! The big challenge she faced was to buy a plot somewhere close to where she was then operating, as the ecosystem was familiar. It also gave her a reasonable chance to divide available time between family and work, while never losing sight of her passionate desire to build a permanent old age home.

After considerable search, she and her friends identified an ideal plot in 2004: the current location of Anandam. She faced great difficulties in raising funds. She organized a rangoli competition and even an event for setting a Guinness book entry. After having identified the land and paying an advance, she applied for approval of the building plans. She and other trustees were clear that there could be no hidden costs, as they were working for a social cause that would create value for society and not for the trust.

In this process, she and her team lost time in making more than 50 visits to various offices for sanction of construction. By the time they finally got it, the project had faced a cost escalation of nearly 100%. Bhageerathy took it as a matter of pride to continue to work hard, instead of compromising on values.

Unblemished love for elders who behave like children: Bhageerathy and her trustees visit the trust several times every day. She has taken voluntary retirement to serve the trust's elderly beneficiaries. She is available on call for any emergency needs. She has gone through counselling courses herself and counsels residents regularly.

As she enters the premises, she addresses someone as "*appa*" (father), another as "*amma*" (mother) and yet another as "*kuzandhai*" (child), spreading affection and love. Residents wait with report cards, seeking attention. She addresses each of them. Presently, the old age home has close to 100 residents in the age group 60-93. The criteria for admission to resident status are that the applicant should be a destitute without support from any relative and with no independent income or wealth to live on. Residents take care of themselves on their own; health, fitness and emotional balance are ensured through exercises, prayers, mentoring and sharing. For her, it is important to treat them with respect and genuine love. It is amazing to see the way she infects them with her boundless energy. She often copes with the realities of conflicting personalities and the need to balance them. One obviously needs a developed sense of family responsibility to drive such a centre.

Keeping in mind the need for healthy food and atmosphere, the centre has a couple, retired from an industrial canteen, who have dedicated themselves to this home by taking care of food preparation. The community celebrates all festivals and national days with fanfare. All residents donate their eyes, and some of them even donate other organs. Thus far, Anandam residents have donated 23 pairs of eyes.

Weaving support: Anandam functions with the active involvement of well-wishers who contribute on their own by sponsoring a meal or something else. Residents are happy folks who jointly share the responsibilities of running the old age home. They spend time sharing common interests and running down their memory lanes. Bhageerathy has encouraged many youth to visit and spend time with the aged people, so that they do not feel completely alienated from society.

Bhageerathy and other trustees have taken the initiative of setting up a hospital for the residents as well as for others in the community to enable them to avail of immediate medical attention. Earlier, they faced huge challenges in responding to health-related emergencies. Now, they manage a team of expert paramedical and medical professionals who support their noble cause. The age factor means that a small number of residents are usually sick, and they are cared for as if they are in a hospital. If at all Anandam can be said to have employees, it is these few medical personnel.

Bhageerathy manages every resident by engaging him or her in some activity. Like a family, every resident takes on some responsibility, such as going out to collect milk from the local vendor's booth, organizing prayers, cutting vegetables and managing the kitchen inventory. Residents take pride in their responsibilities.

A larger initiative that Bhageerathy has undertaken with the help of the TTK Foundation is linking residents with students who want tutoring support in and around the local community. It all started with a resident from southern Tamil Nadu who had been a mathematics teacher handling classes up to the tenth grade. She asked if she could teach some children in the neighbourhood, if that was fine with Bhageerathy. Bhageerathy encouraged her to do so, as the resident would derive positive energy from staying constructively busy. It is now four years since that first start to tutoring children, and the subsequent impact has been phenomenal! TTK Foundation has sponsored a large space in the building with proper lighting and fans, where students of up to the 12th grade come and study between 4.30 and 7.30 p.m. They complete their homework with guidance from the elders, and their academic performance has improved.

Bhageerathy runs this facility absolutely free for beneficiaries. She serves society by using the latent talents and emotional needs of residents to help needy students who cannot afford tuition otherwise but have the strong urge to learn.

Her social leadership traits are evident in her ability to resist the temptation of converting the trust's rapidly appreciating real estate into a quality hospital and learning centre, income from which could enable her to subsidize the trust's activities. Bhageerathy says, "the old age home must evolve as a model centre for destitute folks, so that many more can be replicated in every district by good-hearted individuals". Trustees believe that they hold what society has given to them in trust, and the best way to give it back is with kindness, not though market manipulation.

Conclusion: Bhageerathy believes service with love and affection must flow freely, without any reciprocal expectation, as giving is always a pleasure! Her daughter who is a management graduate is fondly linked to the Anandam residents. Bhageerathy's perseverance, ability to stay positive through all odds and work as part of a team, her charisma and motivation have helped her to be different in serving the cause she holds dear. Many of us would find old age home care a tough proposition, even with a small family. Bhageerathy and her friends are proving to the world that we all can make a difference by extending love and care. We need more of them in society. It is not the physical aspect of setting up old age homes to house the elderly, but the noble aspect of creating a life for neglected elders with nothing to fall back on that makes her a champion!

CHAPTER 23

Relieving the deprived of pain and instilling confidence: Ramakrishnan, Founder President Amar Seva Trust

Mr.Ramakrishnan, President, Amar Seva Trust is receiving
an award in recognition of his service

Introduction: It is a sad reality that some people are born physically challenged. The physical challenges could be deformed limbs, disability in movement or insufficiently developed organs. Physical challenges that come with birth are usually genetic disorders. For the physically challenged, life can be testing, but they usually learn to manage and cope with it over the years. Unfortunately, physically challenged people invariably are confined to a narrow range of activities, and their world view is limited to a small horizon. This kind of confinement usually happens because of their reaction to insensitivity or even outright unkindness from other people, or even because other people actually compel them to stay out of public view as much as possible, because they are seen as liabilities in their families.

In the days before eradication of polio in India, we had the misfortune to see the disease affect many children who landed up becoming physically challenged. In such cases, the disorder occurs at a young age, when the victims will not have experienced much of life; they become physically challenged for life.

Polio has varied levels of impact. Some victims have been fortunate to suffer a limited impact that does not seriously cripple them and allows them to continue with a normal life. In cases where deep infection hampered normal life, there was a system of support available to pursue a near-normal life.

Another category of physically challenged people have the misfortune of being through accidents that physically disable them. The worse cases, of course, are those people who meet with an accident in their prime. There are many examples of young people in their teens losing limbs in accidents. These victims must learn to refocus and rebuild their lives to achieve relative normalcy.

We rarely come across a person who falls in this category, and who not only restructures his life, but also manages to set up an institution to serve the physically challenged. In this write up, we discuss S. Ramakrishnan, the founder of Amar Seva Sangam, who became a quadriplegic in 1975 at the age of 21.

Early days: Ramakrishnan was a brilliant student all through his childhood. He was born in to a middle-class orthodox family at a village called Ayikudy, located in southern Tamil Nadu, an area that was earlier a part of the kingdom of Travancore. After completing his schooling at the Government High School in Ayikudy, he went to Sri Paramakalyani

College, Alwarkurchi, Tirunelveli district, for his pre-university course. He nursed ambitions of graduating in engineering and then serving the country by joining the Defense Services. He joined the Government College of Technology at Coimbatore, where he pursued his engineering studies. In 1975, while he was in the fourth year of his engineering course, he appeared for Defense Services examinations at Bangalore. On the last day of the physical tests, he met with an accident: he fell from a tree. He was rushed to the Air force Command Hospital in Bangalore. After the necessary medical tests, he was found to be affected with quadriplegia—a condition that restricts the ability to function physically, and as a consequence, the person becomes mentally and socially constrained because the spine and other parts of the nervous system connecting the limbs get severely damaged. Ramakrishnan proved this wrong by overcoming physical constraints with extraordinary mental agility and capability to fight in the society for a larger cause.

Initially, Ramakrishnan felt devastated. After four months, he was shifted to the Defense Hospital at Kirkee in Pune for further treatment. He was treated by Dr. Air Marshall Amarjit Singh Chahal; he remained in the hospital until the middle of 1976. When he first came to know of his limitations, he felt miserable and was inconsolable. One can imagine and sympathize with his position. This condition was most unfortunate for a brilliant engineer from a village down south who was aspiring to make a difference in his and others' lives by serving the nation's defense forces and bringing pride and economic well-being to his family.

Incidentally, Ramakrishnan met a Major in the hospital who told him "Once, I had more than 3,000 people reporting to me in a battalion. On a normal day, more than 1,000 people would salute me, but today I am crippled. Instead of looking backwards and lamenting over my misery, I am trying to cope with and face my destiny. I would advise you, Ramakrishnan, to face this reality with courage for the rest of your life".

Ramakrishnan's life turned topsy-turvy, from a brilliant aspiring engineer to a young man confined to his bed, needing support to carry out even the daily routines of life. He returned to Ayikudy intending to spend the rest of his life there.

Return to Ayikudy

Returning to Ayikudy was more a compulsion than a choice. Since the accident had happened during the selection process, he was not eligible for medical support provided to people in confirmed service. He got an opportunity to be at a Red Cross home in Bangalore. However, a Red Cross Sister there advised him that his condition would require a lot of continuous assistance from others even for daily routine, and that as a young man he had to learn to balance his own strong spirit with support from others to fight the disablement. That was when he decided to move to Ayikudy.

Ramakrishnan's physical condition required a separate dwelling unit at Ayikudy. He moved into an old dilapidated house just opposite the house where his family continues to live. One of his classmates from Ayikudy, who had been trained to handle him, became his great supporting pillar. Ramakrishnan had a tough time coping with the reality of his life, as his mind was agile, but his body could not catch up. His constant companion was a transistor, and he spent his time in learning about the world through radio programs.

He used to call out to people who were passing by on the street and chat with them for a while. People often avoided him. To make his life more meaningful, he used to call his three brothers and his sister and help them out with their studies. Slowly, he extended this practice to a few other people in his village. However, for the major part of the day, he felt empty, and his emptiness forced him to feel his helplessness.

Two things happened during this period. One afternoon on a working day, a sympathetic passerby gave him 10 rupees, asking him to buy something useful. This triggered the thought that people empathize with others' inability and help in small ways. He thought, "If my misfortune can make others empathize with me, why don't I create a larger purpose for my life by setting up some enterprise that would benefit other physically challenged people in the region? I see so many of my fellow humans around me who have been affected by polio or have had some disability right from birth through some genetic disorder." It was still like receiving a big favor for a physically challenged person to get a wheel chair and a suitable bed officially sanctioned, as he or she would have to submit an application and go through a lengthy process. This rubbed the emotions and self-respect of physically challenged persons on the wrong side. Ramakrishnan wants to do away with the tears of such people in his region and bring smile on their faces. Now, if we happen to interact with his beneficiaries in Ayikudy, we will experience their unfathomable joy and pride first hand.

As these thoughts were churning deep in him, he heard on the radio that 1981 had been declared the "International Year of the Disabled". Many programs were announced for disabled people through financial support in the form of aid packages and grants. In 1981, Ramakrishnan and a few friends registered his brainchild Amar Seva Sangam under the Tamil Nadu Societies Registration Act, 1975. The organization, named after his doctor and mentor Dr. Amarjit Singh, helps the physically challenged.

Initial years

Ramakrishnan was clear that he would organize polio eradication programs and camps, and provide support for the physically challenged in the region by enabling access to education, skill development and a secured dwelling environment. One can imagine how ambitious such a project was for a wheelchair-bound person who spent a lot of time lying down and seeking help from others for all routine functions. It was not going to be easy to get money to find its way to Ayikudy.

He had a doctor friend who was actively associated with the Rotary Club. This friend had been conducting programs on family planning and health. He offered to help Ramakrishnan. Ramakrishnan also got in touch with Dr. Venkataswamy of Aravind Eye Hospital and Foundation. Dr. Venkataswamy motivated Ramakrishnan to pursue his dreams. He also connected Ramakrishnan to other social activists. Things were not always positive. There were a number of depressing experiences as well. Ramakrishnan recalls how the father of one of his friends coerced him to submit application to five different sources and managed to get paltry support in return. However, this did not dissuade Ramakrishnan as he looked into the positive side of this.

Ramakrishnan decided that he would travel to Chennai to mobilize funds. In Chennai, he stayed at his cousin's house at Valsaravakkam and moved around in a taxi to meet people. He used to leave home by 8 a.m. and had continuous meetings with people until around 3 p.m. After his taxi driver dropped him back home and left, he would freshen up and request his uncles to support him in writing diary and a letter of thanks to all those he met during the day. Many a time, he would not get a hearing from those whom he approached for fund. This never deterred him from his efforts to seek support. This phase lasted 6-8 months in 1990.

A famous author, Siva Sankari, published a five-page story about him titled "Uchi Meethu Vaan Idinthu Veez Kindra Pothilum" in *Ananda Vikatan*. After reading this article, Sulochana from Kolkata sent him a number of letters of encouragement, together with a contribution. She also connected him with the Jindal Trust for further contribution. Ramakrishnan learnt from the Jindal Trust that more than frugality, appropriate utilization is the key to effective use of development finance, and he started using his resources meaningfully. One must understand that he was not an accountant, nor could he afford one. He expanded his tuition centre and Kindergarten to primary school with the funds.

Ramakrishnan got a few introductions and references to great musicians in 1991. He went to a famous Carnatic singer's house, but her secretary advised not to meet as she has become old. However, on seeing Ramakrishnan being moved from his wheel chair to the car, the secretary became compassionate and got an immediate appointment. As Ramakrishnan entered the house to wait for the musician, a female voice welcomed him by name. The lady had heard about him through a known source to her at Ayikudy who used to sympathize with him. He achieved another breakthrough that day when the Carnatic singer and her husband supported him with funds and promised to help him mobilize more funds.

Ramakrishnan used to visit another legendary Carnatic musician. He was not received with kindness, and was given a small amount of money as a token donation. He had to be literally carried from his car to the place of meeting and back. That day, as his driver was carrying him back to the car, he told the legendary singer that he was the grandson of Ayikudy Shri. A.K. Ramakrishnan, a well-known social worker who got facilities like school and hospital for people in and around Ayikudy. After reaching Ayikudy, Ramakrishnan was pleasantly surprised to receive a more substantial financial contribution as well as a commitment to help his cause.

These great musicians encouraged him to organize performances for fundraising. Another well-known musician, Maharajapuram Santhanam, performed at an event.

Humble beginning at Ayikudy

Ramakrishnan bought an old house and refurbished it. He started running support classes at this place for children in his village by appointing a few teachers. He also took in a few physically challenged persons as residents in the house. He started some skill development activities for those who wanted to earn some money for their livelihood. He had surveyed the region with local support, and tried to connect with physically challenged people to encourage them to make use of Amar Seva Sangam.

He used to dream a lot. Sometimes, his associates thought that he was in an imaginary world of his own, and used to spare time to listen to him out of respect and sympathy. He recalls how passionately vice president of Amar Seva Sangam who by profession a mason used to come regularly after dinner at 7.30 p.m. and listen to him until they retired to bed. According to Ramakrishnan, his dreams were real influences in his activities and helped him to be a visionary.

Though his was a visionary effort he managed with strong leadership, it had its own challenges. He required constantly larger investments and organization capabilities to run his services.This resulted in more fundraising trips to different places. Ramakrishnan recalls the support of his driver Ramachandran at Chennai and the emotional bonding that developed between them. Ramachandran was using a cab painted in the traditional dark black and yellow. Security at certain offices did not allow the taxi into the premises. One day Ramachandran did not come to work. Ramakrishnan was worried that Ramachandran had been dissuaded by the limitations on cabs in the name of protocol. The next day he saw, to his surprise, that Ramachandran had repainted his taxi black. He proudly told Ramakrishnan that driving on fundraising activities for a noble cause was more emotionally satisfying than running a commercial taxi. This kind of bondage was important for Ramakrishnan as he continued his struggle towards institution building.

Meanwhile, in 1987 a letter to Sulochana returned undelivered, as the addressee could not be found. This worried Ramakrishnan. To his surprise later, Sulochana connected with Amar Seva and visited them. He came to know then that she is the spouse of a nationalized bank's Chairman.

A friend from Tenkasi and another friend who was his classmate introduced Ramakrishnan to a scientist who was active with the Jaycees in Tuticorin. This scientist gave him and Amar Seva introductions to Jaycees members at the state and the national levels.

Meeting of minds

In 1991, Dr. T.S. Chandra, Professor, IIT, Madras requested Ramakrishnan to come for a meeting with a select audience of members of the Tamil Nadu Physically Handicapped Welfare Association. At an event organized by Amar Seva Sangam following this meet is where Ramakrishnan met the parents of S. Sankara Raman, a chartered accountant who had been physically handicapped by a genetic disorder. They were impressed by the work that Ramakrishnan was doing and told Sankara Raman (whose story I have narrated in another chapter of this book) about it. After a few discussion and visits, Sankara Raman decided to join Ramakrishnan.

Ramakrishnan was particular that Sankara Raman must be comfortable at Ayikudy. They all lived in the same premises and created office space that could help them to be independent and work comfortably on their joint mission. Ramakrishnan being the President of Amar Seva Sangam, focused more on connecting with people and stakeholders, while Sankara Raman worked as the Secretary, with larger operating responsibilities. It may be noted here that even the most professional of organizations often experience severe leadership stress when people of a high caliber and high aspirations come together. One can imagine just how challenging it could have been for physically challenged people with different levels of energy, stamina and agility to come together for a bigger cause. The Ramakrishnan-Sankara Raman team succeeded in overcoming all obstacles because of oneness of purpose.

Family support

Ramakrishnan mentions that everything he achieved became possible only because of the relentless support and confidence boosting given by his parents and siblings. His father always encouraged him to think progressively and face the world with courage. The contributions of his siblings were equally humongous.

Ramakrishnan fondly recollects one particular incident. During the early days of fund raising, he used to reach out to people who were of high standing in society through references. Bharat Ratna C. Subramaniam was a huge supporter of Ramakrishnan's cause. Similarly, he got in touch with a leading cricket star of those days through a reference. The cricketer invited him to Bombay, now called as Mumbai. Ramakrishnan and his brother decided to travel by train to Mumbai. He lacked the confidence to travel far for pursuing this further. He had a temperature and felt sick. His younger brother still wanted him to pursue this journey. His brother had written to his friends at Chennai about their plans. To the surprise of Ramakrishnan, 15 people came to Chennai Railway Station, took him to a hospital and arranged for his treatment. Once he was discharged, they continued onward to Mumbai.

However, the meeting at Mumbai was not fruitful, as the potential donor insisted that the beneficiary had to be a resident of Mumbai. Though Ramakrishnan was disappointed, his brother felt that the experience was a key lesson for them. Building an infrastructure in and around Ayikudy for the benefit of the physically challenged in the region was a dream to translate into reality.

Ramakrishnan is married and his wife supports him strongly. His marriage itself was an interesting turn of event in the life of such an uncommon person. He narrated to the author the first time he heard the voice of his wife in a school music program. He asked her to meet him. Impressed by her desire to teach poor student, he proposed to her in 1986. She asked for time to reply to the proposal, but confirmed her willingness to support him in his endeavors to help the physically challenged achieve independence. Ramakrishnan mentions "She lavished care on me when it was unsolicited! She showed interest in office administration and her contribution was unique in various ways." However, they were able to marry only after a decade.

Ramakrishnan respected the space required for any person to pursue his or her dreams and become independent. He holds the view that it was this attitude that led to his family, friends and the media supporting his endeavors. A number of magazines covered his life story and featured articles on the success of Amar Seva. Awards and accolades are still pouring in. Ramakrishnan does not allow them to sway him away from his goal of helping the physically challenged to live with self-pride and confidence.

Conclusion: Ramakrishnan and Sankara Raman's efforts have culminated in a large organization that touches the lives of thousands of physically challenged people every year. Ramakrishnan's grit and commitment to making a difference to his own life and to those of his fellow physically disabled are phenomenal. The compassion and contribution of good-hearted people in mobilizing resources for a good cause were important in converting his dreams into reality. How much direct help a physically challenged person gets does count, but more important is how much he incorporates social goodwill into his own efforts to become an effective social entrepreneur serving the deprived humans of society. Just think of this: for every Ramakrishnan the society comes out with, the lives of a few hundred or even a few thousand physically challenged people undergo appreciable improvements!

CHAPTER 24

Fighting challenges with dignity and determination: Sankara Raman, Honorary Secretary, Amar Seva Trust

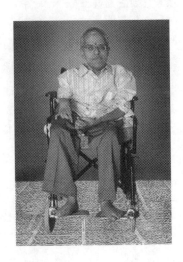

Introduction

One often comes across humans who have disorders derived from hereditary factors. Muscular dystrophy, which refers to a group of hereditary disorder, each with unique phenotypic and genetic features, can cause physical challenges. Congenital muscular dystrophy often appears at birth with hypotonic and severe trunk and limb weaknesses. Obviously, afflicted persons find it difficult to lead a normal life, as they are confined to wheel chairs. Like many other physically challenged people, they also tend to give up enthusiasm and the hope of being a normal human being due to the pains they undergo. This is an undesirable consequence, as they too have the right to lead a normal life.

This is the saga of Sankara Raman, who fought this kind of a physical challenge with courage, determination and intellect.

Early days

Sankara Raman understood his limitations early in life, but did not let it deter him. He always wanted to face the world and lead a complete and independent life. He was afflicted with a hereditary disorder and had a sister who was also crippled. He came from a middle class family and wanted to make a difference to the world, just like any normal youth. The challenges were in getting the right mentor and peer group that would help him fight the limitations imposed by his disorder.

From his earliest days, Sankara Raman was studious. After completing his high school he actively pursued the idea of qualifying as a chartered accountant (CA) so that he could find gainful employment and support his family. He took up graduation in commerce and chartered accountancy. He did the three years articleship under auditor Shivaji in Shivaji and Rao Associates, where he was provided with barrier-free access in office and opportunities without any discrimination in audit assignments. He was never treated as a disabled person and no special privileges were offered which was an eye-opener for him to realize his capabilities and gain confidence. This is a real-time example as to how an employer/senior can motivate a person with disability. He qualified as a CA with a meritorious record and started his practice. He was sure that he wanted to live his life with dignity and contribute to the world by serving other people with similar physical challenges.

During the initial stage of his life, he was unwilling to accept help to overcome his challenges. If anyone offered him support, he was furious. However, his father, who understood him well, helped Sankara Raman to appreciate and accept the need to take others' help whenever it was practical. Once his attitude changed in this manner, Sankara Raman was not only pleased with himself but also made other people around him happy and cheerful. This clear "transformation" laid the basis for what he was to achieve in the later years of his life.

Financial sustainability

We have already mentioned that Sankara Raman did not come from an affluent background. After qualifying as a CA, he faced a further dilemma in deciding just how to pursue his career. One option was to join a corporate and take up a protected life with assured economic status. However, he felt that the corporate sector would see his physical challenge as a limiting factor and would not use him for challenging assignments at work. Hence, he decided that he would not opt for this option, even though it promised financial security.

His father encouraged him to start his own practice as a CA. Sankara Raman faced severe obstacles given his restricted mobility. His professional duties dictated that he travel out of Chennai to towns like Trichy and Salem. He was always dependent on escorts who would accompany him to these places. He had to go through this phase of his life because both financial independence and stability were important necessities at that point of time. He was convinced that being on his own reflected his dignity and his respect for the knowledge he had, which he demonstrated through his commitment to work. From his early stages of life, Sankara Raman held the firm view that a physical challenge can be a limiting factor, but not an intimidating factor that stops someone from leading a normal life.

Ethical values

He had imbibed strong ethical values in his childhood. In professional practice, he faced the normal challenges of society, such as corruption and disability abuse. He felt the best way to handle these challenges was to fight them: abstain from corruption and not allow himself to be marginalized because of physical challenge. On the other hand, he did come across very understanding income tax officers and professionals at the office of the registrar of companies. As time went by, he developed the conviction that his knowledge and ethical values could one day become the key factors that allowed him to pursue his ambition of serving physically challenged fellow beings.

Connecting with peers

Sankara Raman joined the Tamilnadu Welfare Association for Physically Handicapped. He felt the association would not only give him the strength to fight his disorder, but would also enable its members to use different institutions and departments in supporting the community of the physically challenged. At this point, he held the very clear notion that for the physically handicapped, the best way to demonstrate courage would be to fight the negative influences of their handicaps and achieve an independent life. It was preferable to talking on and on about their misfortune and claiming support from private institutions and the government. He also observed that many physically challenged people were refusing to mix with society and were confining themselves to a small circle, cursing their destiny. The obvious reasons were guilt, shame, self-pity and reaction to social cruelty. He felt strongly that these people needed to get over their mental hang-ups, and that they should be given enough encouragement to attain an independent life. Further, physically challenged people needed to adopt a kind of self-confident approach to achieve a normal life, even when using the help of others.

The initiatives of the association were taking shape in the early 1990s. The government allocated some land near Vandalur (a suburb of Chennai) for the association to set up a rehabilitation center. Dr. Varadakutty, president of the association and a few others were having thoughts similar to that of Sankara Raman. He used to spend much of his time with them, working on disability rights, while pursuing his professional practice.

Often, it is hard to make out whether a particular turning point in one's life is destiny, the hand of God or just a random pattern! A turning point came up in Sankara Raman's life. His parents had an opportunity to meet Ramakrishnan of Amar Seva at the residence of Dr. T.S. Chandra, a professor at IIT Madras, in 1991. They were happy with the social service efforts of Ramakrishnan. They encouraged Sankara Raman to meet him. After a few meetings at Chennai and Ayikudy in Tirunelveli district, Sankara Raman was convinced that it would be a good idea to join forces with Ramakrishnan, who was then working on developing his social service organization, Amar Seva, and in setting up a rehabilitation center.

Challenges

Moving to Ayikudy from Chennai was not an easy decision for Sankara Raman. Ayikudy was a small village, and Sankara Raman had to compromise on his professional practice. He had clientele he could not serve from Ayikudy. However, his nature was such that new challenges always attracted him. The best in him comes out when he is most challenged. He accepted the personal challenge of moving into community-based living at Ayikudy. Initially, he shared his time between Ayikudy and Chennai. During this initial period, he had many opportunities to improve the quality of life of the physically challenged, which formed the basis of his ambitious approach to social entrepreneurship in later years.

Sankara Raman always had a thirst for professional knowledge and the gut feeling that knowledge must be used for a decent and respectful lifestyle. Furthermore, one needs to deploy knowledge to enhance the quality of life of the brethren in his community. Whenever there was a need in his community, he never hesitated to take the steps required using the knowledge and momentum he had gained from his interactions with experts in various fields.

Recognition

Sankara Raman was instrumental in incorporating a number of efficient systems into the operations of Amar Seva. These systems helped him considerably in implementing the ideas of the committee members. He recognized the need to demonstrate leadership at operating levels for optimum contribution to social causes. In various ways, he used the experience he had gained with corporate clients when he practiced as a CA. He seized on every opportunity to connect with professionals and associations for improving the programs at Ayikudy. Sankara Raman's zeal and vigor in bringing a structured approach to work is worth emulation by all youth. Sankara Raman says, "Though at the outset it might look compulsive, fighting all odds while depending on physical support from fellow humans to move around is challenging. I always think for what purpose I am doing all these things. If it is purely selfish then it is limiting. If you want to achieve something, you must bring extra energy and spirit to overcome all deterring factors".

Sankara Raman received a lot of support from his family. We have already talked about the major way his parents supported him. His siblings also demonstrated courage and the willingness to fight limitations. His eldest sister had gone trekking in the Himalayas. She went to Canada in 1971 to pursue higher studies and find ways to help the family. She was a great motivator for Sankara Raman. He also has another elder sister, Dr.Sumathi who is afflicted with the same condition, muscular dystrophy. They always thought it fit that they demonstrate extraordinary spirits and individually and jointly contribute to their family and to the larger society. It is worth mentioning here that in fact, Dr. Sumathi is a PhD holder in commerce and plays an active role in the activities of Amar Seva community. She served as a professor in a college at Trichy.

At some point in his life, Sankara Raman felt that he should marry and fulfill his family obligations. He has been married for the last 14 years. He manages to balance the demands of his personal life with those of his developmental work. He encourages his wife to pursue activities of her liking, and likewise, she supports him in his endeavors. My youth readers may note here that it is not just internal understanding that helps harmony, respect for each other's external roles and commitments to those roles matter just as much. Leaders must ensure such practice at home and in the community to achieve a balanced growth.

Conclusion

Sankara Raman has won a number of accolades and awards from national and international organizations. These awards have never swayed him from his purpose. His dream is to spread the loud and clear message that humans who are confined to a wheel chair and dependent on others' help for physical activities can still contribute meaningfully to uplifting their brethren who suffer from similar physical challenges. He is convinced that self-respect and pride in independence in thought and action are vital for fighting physical challenges. So much of the misery on this earth would be mitigated if other people suffering from hardships thought similarly spread awareness! We need more thought leaders like Sankara Raman.

CHAPTER 25

Heart beats for child and women welfare: Raja Panneerselvam, Society for Rural Development Promotion Services

Introduction: There are persons who encounter heavy odds in life at an early age for reasons such as accidents. When they survive such an accident, they find themselves at a crossroads on how they should handle their life going forward. Every now and then, we come across such person who fought great odds and dedicated himself or herself to meaningful social causes.

Early days

Raja Panneerselvam was born in a village in Tiruppatur taluk, Vellore district. He studied till 10th grade in a village school and then went to Tiruppatur for high school education. He obtained his Master's degree in economics in Chennai. Later, he went for a teachers' training course and completed his bachelor's course in education. He later pursued a degree in law as well. This shows the side of his character that valued education as a necessary tool for becoming a good human.

His father was a moral science teacher. He imbibed a high sense of commitment towards society by listening to his father. His mother, who was involved in animal husbandry, also did supportive work at farms. He helped his mother at her work for about six years. While at school, he was studious, but still found time to be active in small saving schemes, capturing historical events and reciting civic stories. He was an active participant in school festivals on occasions such as Independence Day and Teachers' Day. He had a deep interest in philosophy.

Triggers

Two important triggers strongly influenced Raja Panneerselvam to pursue development activities in the later part of his life. The first was an imprisonment while at college and the need to fight a legal case for seven years to clear himself of the allegations. This made him pursue law and understand the rights and duties of a good citizen. He realized that to win justice, one needs to put extra efforts, as the onus of coming out clean lies on the accused or the deprived. This may not be the position everyone adopts, but this is what differentiates Raja Panneerselvam from others.

The second incident happened on December 27, 1989. He was working as a school teacher when he met with an unfortunate road accident. Though he survived the massive crash, he lost his left eye. Normally, a person from such an economic background would have strived for an easy life with the chance to earn a decent living. Instead, he decided that he must commit his future to social service by quitting his teacher's job and serving the needy where he lived.

It was critical for him to continue to receive support from his mother and family to fight setbacks to his pursuit of developmental activities. His mother looked sympathetically at his desire and will to serve the community, and encouraged him a lot. With that encouragement, Raja Panneerselvam got a society registered for rural development promotion services in 1990. This was by no means a small effort for a person born to a middle-class family and aspiring to be independent.

Drive for social cause: In 1990, after recovering from the accident and embarking on his new lease of life, Raja Panneerselvam started the first set of activities at villages near Vaniyampadi by adopting tribal children. Their isolation distressed him, and he involved himself in giving them an identity by putting them through confidence-building exercises. He focused on ensuring basic amenities for them. He represented these students at government offices for getting them ration cards, education and health care. The results of these actions gave him tremendous self-satisfaction and built up his drive to extend his activities. The zeal to help tribal children live a normal life is a noteworthy trait.

He decided to ignore his limitations and extend his social drive further. He started working on HIV AIDS awareness and environment-friendly practices like local organic farming. He used to gather his friends and like-minded people to help him out with his activities. His leadership trait was of great help in enabling him to do so. He held propaganda meetings at street corners, deliver messages through folktales and drama. All these actions look simple and straightforward, yet it was difficult to implement them at ground level.

Raja Panneerselvam was aware of his resource limitations. He thought that the best way to serve economically and socially deprived people was to link up with available state and central government schemes. Not everyone can do this, as it requires in-depth understanding of government machinery and the ability to liaise effectively with officials and persuade them to make things work. Moreover, there were challenges posed by suspicious beneficiaries as well as officials, who had doubts on how he could deliver efficient social service. Raja Panneerselvam spent long hours every day working with the stakeholders concerned to implement afforestation schemes, childcare (day) centres, tribal welfare schemes, rain water harvesting and cleaning of water tanks and *bunds* (embankments and dikes). His beneficiaries were illiterate, necessitating a lot of handholding and patience. He developed a flair for understanding government schemes and taking them to the people—a remarkable leadership trait!

Support of well-wishers: The effects of his accident and the increasing scale of his activities required him to seek the support of other people. Raja Panneerselvam was not in a position to build a social venture or approach funding sources to enable him to augment his human resources. He believed that he had to use the strength of networking to help him out with his cause. Between 1987 and 1991, when he was headmaster of a high school, he had supported 800 poor men and women by giving them opportunities to become qualified teachers in government schools. This was done at a very low cost to them, without expectation of pecuniary return. According to Raja Panneerselvam, 80% of these people were living below the poverty line when he helped them out.

Many of them lived in the areas covered by his operations and were happy to support his cause. This was an appreciable factor in his life as a social worker. It came up mainly because of his nature to do good for people with no return expectations. This made his beneficiaries support him at the most crucial times even when he had not sought any help from them.

Scaling up: One could observe that his engagements increased over time. He had the enthusiasm to scale up his activities, even though factors such as the location, the limited scope for resource mobilization and the need for personal attention, along with his physical limitations, were major challenges. He had the drive to overcome these challenges. Since 1996, Raja Panneerselvam has initiated about 289 women's self-help groups (SHGs). There are about 5,200 members. Many of the member are tribal folks, people living in the foothills, destitute, widows, sex workers, people dependent on forests for livelihood and people who walk long distances because there was a lack of adequate transportation networks.

He started training these women in the three aspects namely reading, writing and arithmetic. He also gave attention to training them in hygiene, in handling atrocities against them and in the evils of female infanticide. He was passionate about spreading his messages on the evils of addiction to drugs, tobacco and liquor. Trafficking of women was a massive problem that victimized innocent women. He was deeply concerned about this menace. He initiated a number of programs to create awareness about the problem, and was personally involved in rescuing women who had been trafficked. He facilitated these SHGs to mobilize Rs. 36 crores of loan, use the proceeds profitably and efficiently repay the entire amount. Instead of looking at these achievements as mere activities of social workers or chores of NGOs, one must see them against the backdrop of Raja Panneerselvam and his determination to fight the limitations imposed on him by his accident. One can then observe his deep desire to work for deprived, directionless and unfortunate women who were being exploited by antisocial elements.

Raja Panneerselvam started focusing on taking his involvement in social service to a higher level. This necessitated the creation of a core facility from where he could operate. He had been deeply concerned about the injustice prevailing in the region (like in so many other parts of the country), especially injustice directed at children and women. His primary activities included fighting female infanticide, raising a voice against atrocity towards women, rehabilitating women involved in trafficking, supporting destitute women and women who were mentally ill due to abduction and forced sex work. In the following paragraphs, the author documents Raja Panneerselvam's determination to fight injustice against child and women.

In 2000, Raja Panneerselvam built the headquarters for all the activities of his society at Tiruppatur in Vellore district. It provided 24-hour care. Between 2001 and 2003, his focus was on raising HIV/AIDS awareness among women engaged as sex workers. He encouraged them to give up their profession, join the social mainstream and live with dignity. According to him, the society he leads interacts with about 800 sex workers every year, attempting to change their mindsets and to bring them back into the mainstream of society.

In 2004, he increased his scope of activities, under a central government scheme to support destitute women and children. He focused on training women to be self-employed and live independently. They were then moved back to live in society. He has helped nearly 70 women through this scheme in Tiruppatur. During a period of about four years, he rescued 24 infant girls and entrusted them to care under the government's cradle scheme.

Attention to children: Since 2007, he has been running a centre for rehabilitation of orphaned children at Tiruppatur. He helps to get them adopted by eligible couples. Even though female infanticide rates are reportedly coming down as people get more educated on the appalling nature of such crimes, incidences still happen. Abandoned girl children are found in or near garbage bins, bus stops and depots, canal banks, hospital corridors and police stations. He has set up a system whereby he receives messages about abandoned girls through informers and rushes to rescue them. According to him, some children are even attacked and injured by street dogs before he retrieves them. His challenge is to lead them back to a normal life with adequate nutrition and health quotient. Furthermore, he is able to achieve only a small part of what he desires, as there are physical limitations to communication and synchronization of activities. He has extended his operations to beyond Vellore district, covering Tiruvallur, Villupuram, Tiruvannamalai and Cuddalore districts. He shows his tremendous resolve by taking personal care to save every abandoned child.

This is challenging work in terms of the effort, time and diligence required. The processes are rightly stringent. Raja Panneerselvam brings extraordinary humanity to the whole process, in which there is no commerce involved. It is a matter of resurrecting the life of a child and possibly later, a couple and that child, and of harmonizing the relationship through mentoring—something that is key to success. One would understand the depth of effort involved only when one probes into every activity involved in the process of getting a child cleared for placement and then finding the right couple. The activity requires clearly demarcated areas, staff and medical care for the children. Even though most centres of this sort do yeomen service by resurrecting children and make couples happy, Raja Panneerselvam's passion in this service as well as his other activities is phenomenal.

All these activities require extensive record keeping; the documentation part has to be handled with great care to validate the quality of care and attention given to beneficiaries. He personally supervises all these activities. Though it takes time in terms of recording, maintaining and filing reports and returns with the government, this is critical for sustaining the operation.

Similarly, under another scheme called Gokulam Home for Children, launched by the government of India in 2000, he runs a home for resurrecting children whose parents ignored and disowned them and homeless orphans who have been surviving by begging on trains and streets. He approaches the courts to bring these children home and send them to school. Currently, he serves 15 girl children and one male child under this scheme. These activities show his passion for children's well-being.

He runs a program to educate adolescent girl children on the need to be safe and careful against likely offenders, and equip them to protect themselves. He conducts workshops once in a quarter. He has a wide network of friends who are auto drivers, petty shop owners, teachers and local leaders in villages and assist in running these programs by acting as torchbearers for protecting young girls. The leadership shown by Raja Panneerselvam is appreciable.

Spreading wide: Along similar lines, he retrieves trafficked women as soon as he gets information on them. He then communicates with the appropriate authorities in each woman's home state to coordinate the work of placing them back in society. This again requires personal attention and care from him. This project comes under UJJAWALA, the Comprehensive Scheme for Prevention of Trafficking and Rescue, Rehabilitation and Re-Integration of Victims of Trafficking for Commercial Sexual Exploitation, under the supervision of the Ministry of Women and Child Development. While he conducts all these activities through his registered society, he is operationally responsible and needs to involve himself.

Conclusion: We have observed that Raja Panneerselvam has showed tremendous courage in fighting for justice. His physical impairment due to an accident has not deterred him, but rather, drives his passion. His upbringing and ingrained nature of carrying out benevolent services facilitated him to strengthen his focus. His passion has been to fight against female infanticide and injustice against children and women. Operating in a backward district and a small town, he needs a lot of energy and drive to pursue his passion. He does not have the money or stature to attract professionals to work with him. However, these limitations never stopped him; some of his activities even go beyond his local area. Avoiding any temptation to attract funds, he stays focused on his deeds, impacting the beneficiaries directly. Here is a man who has stood tall against all odds and worked to make women and children safe and secure from atrocities. Wish that there were more such men so that women and children would be happy and peaceful on Indian soil!

CHAPTER 26

Doing a little more in making life meaningful: Jolly Johnson, Executive Director, Helping Hands Organization

Introduction: While at school, most of us would have done some service as an engagement option to pass time or as a compulsive engagement for certification by the NSS or the NCC. A few of us get moved by social needs and want to pursue options that are more meaningful to society. Some think of becoming doctors, because their dreams revolve around curing the illnesses of people. For others, the inner desire could be establishing economic justice and even social justice by becoming a lawyer. Yet others would be determined to become teachers and educate children. The list of options goes on. However, all these categories of student ambitions are looked at as career options rather than as social activities. Rarely do we come across a person who wants to become a social activist at a very tender age, during school life. It is more normal they relate with one of the religious congregations as out of faith rather than from a desire to serve.

Jolly Johnson is one such person who showed traits of becoming a social activist and started pursuing this line right from school, which was quite different from what most of the students of her time wanted to do. She showed an exemplary nature in donating a wheel chair to someone who needed it from her pocket money when she was at school. In this chapter, we will see how she has taken to social work over the years and what have been a few defining moments in her life.

Early days: Jolly was born at Thiruvananthapuram to an orthodox family. From childhood, her parents helped her to build relationships with society and extend love and affection to elders. She liked the challenges of study and at the same time, was involved in a number of club activities, engaging with peer-level students and her immediate ecosystem in small and meaningful ways. Private schools offered many opportunities for children pursuing such engagements. On the other side of the coin, there are schools where such opportunities were not so freely available. Jolly focused more on engaging with children in the latter class of schools. She carried on with this even when she went for her college education.

She was full of the spirit to help peer children, especially when they were from low-income groups. She taught students in batches of 2-32 when she herself was in school. This was not for pocket money but was purely out of a sense of service. The students she helped did not have adequate support at their homes and could not afford private tuition. She was helping 54 students even as she was studying for her higher secondary level exams. To me, this was a phenomenal effort by someone to treat their own study priorities at par with the study priorities of peers from less affording segments. Unless someone is truly altruistic, such demeanor is impossible.

She graduated as a bachelor of science in botany. Then she went on to pursue her master's degree in sociology and business administration. As a student, her strength was in the sciences; while as a person, her strength lay in relating with people. The latter strength is what led her into social work. When the author asked her whether she wanted to become a doctor and serve people, she mentioned that she could never nurture such a thought as she was focused on each day's happenings and on being happy. If she had been more self-centred, she might have accomplished that too.

Triggers: Jolly runs an NGO named Helping Hands Organisation (H2O) with a vision to create a better world for the deprived and the needy. The special focus is on differently abled children. Jolly works on three distinct areas, namely, assistance for differently abled children, for destitutes and for the ill, suffering in their dwellings. These services have come out of her conviction on the need to support people in distress.

First, she was deeply disturbed by a child who was afflicted with cerebral palsy and donated a wheel chair. This happened when she was in school, as mentioned earlier. She was moved by a number of differently abled children in her locality. Developed nations have policies and practices to detect such problems early and work on providing support to reduce the severity of the consequences of crippling. Jolly felt that parents in India can be helped with early detection of health issues with their children and further, that children affected can be better trained to handle their lives. She also noticed that parents in India have a tendency to be naïve and less courageous in facing the reality, as culturally they were conditioned not to do anything till their children reached a certain age. One may think of this mindset as due to religious sentiments or belief in pre-ordained destiny. However, the result of this mindset is that affected children are not getting the desired share of assistance. Jolly felt that she must intervene in such cases.

Second, Jolly and her friends, as a group, generally believed in doing a little more; as a regular policy, they kept buying extra consumer durables during their purchases and pooling them, so that over time there was enough to distribute to the needy. Jolly and her friends in the college visited an old age home. Suddenly, one old lady hugged her and started crying inconsolably. Jolly also cried out of reactive emotion; she was deeply touched, as the woman was not in full control of her senses and had been treated as a lost person. On probing further, Jolly came to know that the lady had been picked up from a train after it had reached its destination. She did not know what to do then. She was able to communicate her plight and later landed up at the home with the assistance of railway authorities and social workers. The lady addressed Jolly as her daughter. Jolly was moved that the lady expressed relief that she found her daughter. It was rather like a scene in a melodramatic Indian movie! It made a permanent impact on Jolly. Jolly used to visit that lady regularly. She would demonstrate ecstasy by singing and dancing with her. During one of her visits, the lady, who was holding her hand, breathed her last, bidding "good bye".

Opportunities for service: Jolly saw opportunity in serving differently abled children. She worked on understanding her own strengths and limitations in taking up such an initiative. After a number of interactions, she decided that she would work for improving the lot of children affected by autism. She has a centre at Kariavattom, Thiruvananthapuram, where she addresses the needs of children from two to nine years of age. She regularly interacts with their parents on how to address socio-cultural issues. Many times, autism stays undetected till very late in children; once it is identified, it is not accepted as a reality that demands support. She rightfully feels such an approach cripples affected children and inhibits their ability to handle the challenge as time progresses. "Inadequate infrastructure and lack of parents' initiative should not be limiting for a child who may not deserve such pains" is what Jolly mentions. Noble thinking indeed! She has enough experience at microlevel when she mentions this. When she decided to intervene, she called on 58 parents, based on data sourced from local administration. Only four of them first responded to her seeking support. She feels this is a distinctive cultural lacuna compared to the Western world, where people want to address the problem upfront. This is not a judgment of what is right or what is wrong. It is an effort to bring about an attitudinal change on accepting reality and seeking support to remedy a hard situation.

In a different interaction, the author came across a crippled child who mentioned that her own siblings believed her crippling was a divine choice and pre-ordained misfortune. She did not get adequate recognition and help in approaching life with confidence. Finally, she decided to take the support of an NGO.

Now, a couple of years later, Jolly has 47 children in her centre, of whom 22 have learning disabilities. As the children are categorized on the basis of the severity of affliction, Jolly is of the opinion that if the malady is addressed on time, children with mild and medium autism can be enabled to have a near-normal life. However, such an approach requires the right intervention in adequate measures.

On providing support to the sick and the destitute, Jolly does a phenomenal service, considering her age and background. Elderly people who are bedridden receive special medical care, nutritional food supplements, cots, clothing, mattresses, wheelchairs, hearing aids, calipers, etc., whenever needed. She has been extending this support over many years after her encounter with the women mentioned earlier. It is very difficult to think of the plight of so many destitute folks who were disowned by their own children and siblings. At all times, it cannot be anything but cruel that elders are together fending for themselves under tough conditions. Jolly mentioned an encounter in a dwelling where she saw an old man suffering from hyperglycemia. He had vision impairment and was unable to move around, as his limbs were severely affected. As Jolly moved into the dwelling, she saw his wife, who was completely crippled because of gangrene in her legs. Further into the dwelling, Jolly came across the lady's elder sister, who was chronically ill. The plight of these people was completely inhuman. Jolly and her team are now supporting this family. She cites so many other similar interventions. Though there are some forms of support available through public systems, afflicted people are not able to approach these systems. Jolly and her team attend to around 270 people; each individual visits 11 people in a day and tries to see everyone at least twice a month.

Challenges: There are some challenges to going ahead with these services at a scale that can bring significant impact. The first is the financial challenge. Jolly has put all her earnings into this project. After her college, she decided to work in an agricultural estate as Head of Human Relations, wherein she attended to the socioeconomic needs of 250 workers and their families. She was managing her social work along with her professional work and was using her earnings to hire volunteers to handle her work in delivering services. At some point, this became difficult, and she had to quit her job to be a fulltime social worker. She leveraged the support of her friends and family. Jolly got married about a year and half back. Her spouse encouraged her to work full time on her social endeavors and their families are now supporting her to a reasonable extent. However, she is looking at a sustainable model where grants and aid along with some operational income can help to achieve an appreciable size of operations.

She is enterprising, and has the vision to impact her work through some philanthropists by creating a community of social workers who would be living in an appropriate place, so that children in whom autism has been deducted early can be brought there along with their families. This would help give them fulltime attention so that they get cured and are back into a near-normal stream.

To get operational income, she goes around extensively selling crafts created by such people, either in her organization or through other similar NGOs. She has greater plans for setting up outlets for such products so that their proceeds can enable the less privileged to get better help.

Another challenge she faces is attracting volunteers to work as she scales up. Obviously, any startup, including the commercial and business ones, finds it difficult to attract human resources. One can imagine the plight of startup social organizations. She is spreading her activities into different zones. She has to meet volunteers and make them interact in peer groups. Today, she literally uses public places like parks to enable her volunteers to meet in a central location for sharing experiences and resolving issues with support for delivery of service. The author is not sure how many young postgraduates in management and other business-related subjects can even think of scaling up operations like this. Jolly's enterprising leadership is what keeps her volunteers motivated.

However, like any other business, her initiatives would attract funds on merit, as social capital providers look at fund utilization, leadership and professionalism as important criteria in making decisions to provide capital.

Conclusion: It is rare to come across a youth who has taken up social work as a choice at a prime age, with the intention of impacting her immediate society. It is not her own suffering in any form that forced her to do something like this. Her ability to look at those suffering as her own people and her deep desire to impact them positively with service from childhood are worth emulating by all other youth. The joy and satisfaction that Jolly derives is immense. Education and grooming give clarity of thought and passion to make a difference to people around you who are deprived. It is not enough to give financial support. There must be a set of people who act on the ground. It is not possible for local administrations to cover all those who are deprived. Like Jolly and her H2O, one must see the trigger in oneself to serve and light the spark for betterment of society. The attitude of "doing just a little more" can make the world around us better!

CHAPTER 27

Conclusion

The Incredible Champions we have discussed in this work have treaded uncommon paths, each in his or her own way, to bring about a significant and meaningful impact on society. The champions we have discussed represent different age profiles: as young as the 20s to as old as the early 80s. They come from different socioeconomic backgrounds. They also have different educational credentials. They have been groomed in their early stages of life in distinctively unique circumstances. All of them have something common—the deep desire to touch and benefit the lives of humans, making the world around better for everyone.

The Beginning: If we look at when the champions we have discussed started social work, we find ourselves with a mysterious question to answer. People such as Dr. Balasubramaniam, Arun Krishnamurthy, Jolly Johnson and Saravanan started early in life. Activists such as Padmini Gopalan took to a new social activity in their early seventies. Benefactors such as Deepa and Jayanthi started in their middle age, after having moved to an advanced stage in family life and with the full support of their families. Hence, it can be concluded that age does not matter. Probably, what actually matters is the trigger that drives a deep desire to be different and make a difference through social work.

Actors at Social Work: Before getting into the thick of action, let us look at the actors themselves. Here again, we come across champions who have taken up social work as their fulltime activity by converting their passion into a continuous social improvement engagement, on which they depend for their livelihood. For example, Balasubramaniam started pursuing his social work plan right from his medical education days, when he had already dedicated himself to serving poor people. The same is true of Saravanan, Manoharan, Ramakrishnan, Shankar Raman, Narayanan Krishnan and Shadab Hassan.

We also come across a category of professionals who start social work as a distinct, responsible activity that, along with their livelihood engagements, involves substantial commitment. This set of professionals from our study includes Arun Krishnamurthy, Rajkumar, Bhageerathy and Vazir. But the fact is that it can be a substantial engagement, if with one's livelihood elsewhere. Smart professionals can use their work environment for serving the social cause.

There is another category of professionals who have taken to social work at a different stage in life. These actors are probably driven by a deep sense of the need to do something different and to be unique to society. This would include professionals like Padmini Gopalan, Raja Paneerselvam and Jayanthi Ramesh.

The following diagram depicts the same.

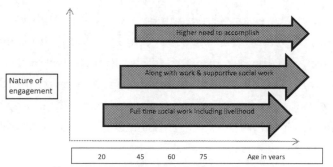

To summarize the age and choice of engagement aspects, neither

To summarize the age and choice of engagement aspects, neither is a limiting factor for someone to commit his or her time, energy and resources to improving the lot of society. One may start one's career life as a social worker and build a career around it. One may have an employment and still take up social work as an additional activity, while still remaining passionate to contribute to the society. Finally, one might have reached a higher level of hierarchy as in Maslow's theory and look for self-actualization. One may take up work that brings meaning to society after having peaked in one's career. Peaking in a career is not in the general perception. It is one's own judgment as to what the limit is of a career or a life. It is important to note that it is not when that matters. The choice to structure one's engagement is what makes one a champion. I am not saying that coming out as the winner of a championship is the end destination one should aim at. I would rather say that it is a state of contentment, and the satisfaction of giving to society in a meaningful way is what matters. If individuals and professionals understand, appreciate and apply themselves, they will leave the world around better than when they came into it.

Choice of Social Engagement: If one were to draw inferences from the Champions we have discussed about what one must be most engaged with, one may again have to go back to the trigger behind social work. But by and large, there is a large scope for certain guidelines to choose an area of work. Our champions have chosen to work in areas such as education, health care and environment for sustainability. In the previous stage of development of our economy, food, housing and clothing were given the highest priority, especially for downtrodden and deprived sections of the society who could not, on their own, afford such essentials. Hence, most government programs were focused on improving these facets of needs. Even today, some government programs continue to cater to the same requirements.

The next levels of requirement for the young as well as the aged populations are education and health care. Though the government focuses on these needs, it is important that development workers ensure the efficacy of investment to these sectors by providing exemplary leadership. They also need to demonstrate the traits of objectiveness, fairness and truthfulness. One must see way beyond one's own self-interests to be able to maintain the social fabric necessary for sustainability of cultural and social values. When we discuss these perspectives, we must also remember that social sensitivity includes the need to address the sustainability and longevity of Mother Earth for future generations as well. Thus, there is a wide and meaningful structured menu of development works a social entrepreneur can choose from.

Common Traits

It is further interesting to note the following most commonly found traits:

1. Groom appropriately
2. Build and play as a part of a team
3. Maintain dedication to stay put against all odds, including financial stress
4. Stay disciplined to the core and stick to the purpose
5. Maintain high energy levels for long and sustained efforts day in and day out
6. Lead from the front during tough times
7. Sustain the passion and obsession for making a difference
8. Stay persuasive even against common thinking and beliefs
9. Become the prodigy of a suitable, committed mentor
10. Reach out far and wide to translate a vision into an action plan and deliver consistently for upliftment of the society.

After close interactions with the professionals who are engaged with social work, I have found that they all had most of these traits in common.

Understanding the trigger factor

Finally, it may be worth mentioning here that to become one of these champions, we must understand how a trigger works and the internal thought and feeling processes that are involved in creating a sustainable plot and in executing the same. For some social entrepreneurs, the trigger could be a sheer accident or a chance factor that had a deep impact on them. We saw this in the cases of the late Manoharan, Murali, Raja Paneerselvam and for that matter, even in the case of someone like Jayanthi Ramesh. If it comes about at all, you will recognize that incident in your life that changes it forever. If there is a carving in your life, follow your instinct with grit, and take the support of mentors to make your act meaningful.

For some others, the trigger could be because of in the influence of so-called environmental factors, that is, social, economic and cultural factors. These factors could have constituted a limitation to proper schooling and education or health care. A victim of one or more of these limitations may fight hard against them, and decide to facilitate other people who are in similar situations to get out of them.

The case of Saravanan, who works for educating tribal and remote area children, is highly instructive: he makes it clear that in order to achieve high-order goals, you need not be aged, highly educated or from a high strata of society.

Sometimes, the trigger could arise from a moving instance a person faces in his or her life, radically changing his or her own life to rally around a cause. This can be seen from the actions of Fr. Thomas, Narayanan Krishnan and Dr. Balasubramaniam. This kind of stimulus could hold for someone like G.V. Subramanian, who was influenced to leave a comfortable job to deliver something that he perceived to be important for making his life complete. All these people have shown tremendous fortitude and determination we have discussed earlier.

Sometimes, the trigger could simply be the values and beliefs a person is brought up with, which at some point in time result in the articulation of a plan to be executed over a period of time. Sometimes, there is a refinement of intellectual thinking, or what one would call a flash of wisdom, to carve out something meaningful to the society. It is not the size of the impact but the quality of the service that is important.

I am not being judgmental, nor am I articulating or prescribing social acts for achieving self-actualization. But I strongly believe that society needs you as much as anyone else to help our fellow humans live an honorable and meaningful life. After all, we owe it to ourselves and to society to contribute to a pleasant, loving and harmonious living. In fact, some of our champions have gone beyond the lives of humans in giving them honor and dignity in death as well.

About the Author

N Chandrasekaran

N Chandrasekaran has a Ph.D in Financial Management (1990), Institute for Financial Management and Research, University of Madras. He has a vast corporate and academic experience in areas relating to Corporate Planning, Strategic Management, Mergers, Acquisitions, Organization Development and Supply Chain. He is also a Certified Supply Chain Professional (CSCP), Association of Operations Management, USA.

He is currently with Take Solutions Ltd as Vice President – Corporate Affairs and serves as Director, Centre for Logistics and Supply Chain Management, Loyola Institute of Business Administration, Chennai. Chandrasekaran has worked for agro based business for organizations like National Dairy Development Board, sugar business of leading groups, and with IT and knowledge based companies as Head of Strategy, Human Resources Management, and Policy and Systems.

He has authored a book on Supply Chain Management published by Oxford University Press of India in 2010. He has jointly authored a book on Strategic Management published by Oxford University Press of India in 2011. He has jointly authored a book on Agribusiness Supply Chain Management which is published in 2014 by Taylor & Francis, New York, U S A. He has also published a work on "Ethical Supply Chain Management in India" in 2012. He has published a number of articles in leading professional journals and authored case studies. He works with Startups, mentors professionals and first generation entrepreneurs. He is active with industry bodies in areas relating to higher education, development research, human development and areas relating to Corporate Social Responsibility.

ABOUT THE BOOK

Incredible Champions brings out how various professionals who are contributing significantly to the society have gone about doing the same. This book takes through experiences and journey of the champions to illustrate and define the various issues of social sector in India. It explains how exemplary professionals see opportunity in challenging times and circumstances to serve a larger society. Whether it is work of Narayanan Krishnan serving the destitute or that of Dr. Sai Lakshmi working for children from deprived economic community or that of Dr. Balasubramaniam serving the tribal for better health care and education, the objective remains the same—trying help humans around us experience a better living. Case studies are spread across age group, from professionals in early 20s to those who are in advanced stage in career. Similarly, number of years has not been used as criteria for choosing a professional to be profiled. But inspirational line of service and commitment has been highlighted. The author has tried to cover all the important aspects of trigger to get involved in this sector, opportunities and challenges. There seems to be some common traits in spite of unique works. These include: determination, grit, humbleness, ability of not succumbing to pressure and work with resolute and so on. The readers would find it useful to know how important it is to relate to the society. Moreover, as Indian companies focus on contributing to social capital for committing to "Corporate Social Responsibility of Business", they can see enough scope for their engagement.